What People Are S

Those of us who are committed through various disciplines to healing in relationships know what a significant breakthrough comes when we can help people recognize the distinct "selves of the self" that are always in play. *Bring Yourself to Love* is a warm and persuasive invitation to undertake this breakthrough, and because it isn't complicated or daunting it will be a tool for insight and change that many different kinds of people will appreciate.

—THE REV. MARTIN L. SMITH, SPIRITUAL TEACHER IN
THE EPISCOPAL CHURCH, AUTHOR OF
A SEASON FOR THE SPIRIT

Dr. Mona Barbera brings clarity and wisdom to the Internal Family Systems governing couples relationships. By naming the parts of the system, couples are able to understand their purpose and power. *Bring Yourself to Love* empowers couples to understand their frustrations and use the relationship to heal their partner and their self, and learn the power of "giving better back." This book is a gem among relationship books.

—WADE LUQUET, PH.D., ASSOCIATE PROFESSOR OF
SOCIOLOGY & HUMAN SERVICES AT GWYNED-MERCY
COLLEGE, AUTHOR OF *SHORT-TERM COUPLES
THERAPY: THE IMAGO MODEL IN ACTION*

Mona Barbera's new book, *Bring Yourself to Love,* presents a unique and hopeful approach to addressing both the day-to-day and problematic aspects of intimate relationships, and to promote connection and understanding. Her approach is inviting, engaging, and non-blaming; the use of the Internal Family Systems model as a framework for understanding and resolving both internal and external polarizations is a true contribution to the field of couples therapy!

—RALPH S. COHEN, PH.D., LMFT, DIRECTOR OF
THE MARRIAGE AND FAMILY THERAPY PROGRAM
AT CENTRAL CONNECTICUT STATE UNIVERSITY
AND IFS LEAD TRAINER

Mona Barbera's new book offers partners a compassionate way to view and address their own and their mate's repeated neurotic reactions. Instead of falling into despair when the same old argument surfaces, Barbera offers a practical system for elevating it to an exercise in intimacy.

—SUSAN PIVER, AUTHOR OF *HOW NOT TO BE AFRAID OF YOUR OWN LIFE*

This captivating book by Mona Barbera, Ph.D., is a must read for couples and therapists everywhere. Inside its covers, the reader finds principles and tools that led Mona herself, and her many couples, from a land of injury and pain into a place where connection and aliveness easily emerge. Dr. Barbera's personal and professional journey is way beyond wonderful and a gift to us all.

—SUNNY SHULKIN, LCSW, BCD, FACULTY, INSTITUTE OF IMAGO RELATIONSHIP THERAPY

I love *Bring Yourself to Love*! Mona's approach and style is so accessible that I was able to apply it to my own life immediately. This book is about helping us grow up and love the way we have wanted to, but have been unable to, because of the many "parts" that live in us, unreconciled.

—MARILYN PAUL, PH.D., AUTHOR OF *IT'S HARD TO MAKE A DIFFERENCE WHEN YOU CAN'T FIND YOUR KEYS*

Whereas many self-help books only highlight the importance of changing oneself in order to change one's relationship, Mona Barbera, Ph.D., in her excellent new book, actually demonstrates how to go about doing this. *Bring Yourself to Love: How Couples Can Turn Disconnection into Intimacy* is a wonderful, practical, and easy to read book with very helpful exercises. This book is in alignment with the values of GoodTherapy.org and will benefit many couples who want to strengthen their relationship or save their marriage.

—NOAH RUBINSTEIN, LMFT, EXECUTIVE DIRECTOR OF GOODTHERAPY.ORG

Dr. Barbera's book is an eminently readable roadmap that guides couples through the challenging terrain of their relationships. Using easy to understand yet very important concepts of their inner lives, Dr. Barbera helps them navigate the dark valleys and parched deserts so they can again find the oases and mountain tops of love. A must resource for couples and all clergy who work them.

—Rev. Dr. Ed Babinsky, United Church of
Christ Minister, East Longmeadow, MA

Bring Yourself to Love is a beautifully written book with an invitation for couples to reframe their relationships through the lens of Internal Family Systems therapy. Mona Barbera offers explanations and very understandable exercises for couples to explore relationship dynamics without judgment of themselves or their partners. It speaks directly to the core of human longing for love and connection, and offers hope for partners to learn how to change negative cycles of behaving and relating into positive interactions.

—Toni Herbine-Blank, MS, RN, CS-P, Senior
Trainer, Internal Family Systems

Every so often an invaluable book comes a long. When I find a book like that I keep a pile at my office to give to clients. *Bring Yourself to Love* is one of those books. Written for couples, the material is helpful for people in any kind of relationship. I've been loaning my copy to people who are working out issues with their bosses, work colleagues, friends, and yes, their significant others. They come back telling me about their relief, saying the book is easy to understand, easy to use, simplifying complex relational dynamics. Now, that's the book to keep around!

—Deirdre Fay, MSW, author of *Becoming
Safely Embodied* Skills Manual

I enjoyed and learned so much from this book. It is excellent. . . so clear, compassionate and helpful and from such an experienced place.

—Shelley Hartz, RN, MSN, CS

I have known Mona for many years, and have always admired her sharp intellect. It is a joy to now experience her brilliance in a useable form. *Bring Yourself to Love* provides a user-friendly format for accessing the best in ourselves and in all our relationships. I can't (thankfully) keep my copies in my office; both clients and I feel very grateful to Mona for creating this book.

—CHRISTINE MATHNA, M.A., IFS LEAD TRAINER,
CONFERENCE PRESENTER

Bring Yourself to Love not only has deep, important concepts— like "giving better back" and "if it's intense it's yours," but it's also very user-friendly. I really like it, and I recommend it to therapists and clients alike. It is a helpful companion on the journey of self-knowledge through relationship. Mona brings herself, personally and professionally, into the teaching offered in this book, creating a rich heart-centered experience.

—CINDY LIBMAN, LICSW, LMFT, CAEH

Written with compassion, wisdom and conviction, *Bring Yourself to Love* is a user-friendly guide (complete with worksheets and exercises) for couples who wish to heal their relationship. It is an equally clear introduction for clinicians who want to apply Internal Family Systems theory and technique in their couples practices. Many of us learned years ago that ego-state work could contribute to therapeutic success, and we have been fascinated to learn about the developments introduced by Richard Schwartz in his IFS theory. In this book experienced couples therapist Mona Barbera has truly done justice to the IFS model. She invites us on a new and exciting path to helping couples create and sustain deep and loving connection.

—RHONDA L. SABO, PSY.D., PSYCHOTHERAPIST AND
FORMER PRESIDENT, NEW ENGLAND SOCIETY FOR
THE TREATMENT OF TRAUMA AND DISSOCIATION

As a demographer focusing on couples and reproductive health, I am aware of the very high rate of divorce in the U.S., and the high number of births (37%) to unmarried women. It seems that when many couples encounter major difficulties in the relationship, instead of working hard to resolve the differences, they opt for the individualistic response of dissolving the relationship. Mona Barbera's book gives theoretical background and lots of practice exercises for those couples committed to working together toward understanding each others' inner selves and how they sometimes lead them to hurt and defensiveness. "Giving better back" is a beautiful starting point for healing relationships.

—STAN BECKER, PROFESSOR, DEPARTMENT OF
POPULATION, FAMILY AND REPRODUCTIVE
HEALTH, JOHNS HOPKINS UNIVERSITY

With the disarming love that permeates IFS, Mona Barbera discerns the inner architecture of intimate relationships. She provides a well-built jungle gym on which to test and develop relational muscles, and a breathtakingly simple path to creating and sustaining sane, loving relationships.

—DAVID STERN, PSY.D.,
PSYCHOTHERAPIST AND AUTHOR

Bring Yourself to Love

BRING
YOURSELF
TO LOVE

How Couples Can Turn Disconnection into Intimacy

Mona R. Barbera

DOS
MONOS
PRESS

Book Cover Design: Accurance
Illustrations by Digications and Aaron Fox
Interior Design: Woodhaus Studio
Index: Christine Frank

Library of Congress Catalog Number: 2015934640
ISBN 13: 978-1-934787-04-5
ISBN 10: 1-934787-04-3
Printed in the United States of America
10 9 8 7 6 5 4 3 2 1
Published by Dos Monos Press
341 Broadway, Providence, RI 02909

First Edition 2008 | Second Edition 2016
Printed in the United States of America

Barbera, Mona R., author.
    Bring yourself to love : how couples can turn
    disconnection into intimacy / Mona R. Barbera. -- Second edition.
    pages cm
    LCCN 2015934640
    ISBN-13: 978-1-934787-04-5
    ISBN-10: 1-934787-04-3

    1. Marriage. 2. Married people. 3. Man-woman
    relationships. 4. Communication in marriage.
    5. Intimacy (Psychology) 6. Problem solving.   I. Title.

    HQ734.B2425 2015   306.81
                           QBI15-1404

Disclaimer
Bring Yourself to Love: How Couples Can Turn Disconnection into Intimacy is a resource for persons interested in couple relationships. Its sole claim is to provide a theoretical perspective, and through a variety of procedures, to introduce interested persons to a process of relationship growth. It is not offered as and does not constitute psychological advice. A psychologist-client relationship is not established by the use of the content of this book. You should consult a licensed professional regarding any specific issues you have.

For my husband, Monk

Table of Contents

List of Exercises

Foreword

I will never forget the experience of calling Mona Barbera in to consult on a couple I was seeing. They both had parts that seemed totally committed to their moral struggle, sparing no effort in their attempt to demonstrate how they were each innocent victims of the other's unjust and malicious behavior.

After they each eloquently stated their case, the husband told Mona, with skepticism dripping from his voice, "Michael claims we are each fifty percent responsible for our problems" with the clear intention of going on to prove how his wife was, in fact, ninety-nine percent at fault.

Mona interrupted him and said that she also strongly disagreed with me. That got his attention and he stopped talking. After a skillfully timed pause, Mona said she believed that they were both one hundred percent responsible for healing their relationship, and that at any moment either of them could choose to turn it into something more connected and satisfying.

She then outlined for them the brilliant and powerful concepts you will find in Chapter 6: that each of them has the option at any moment to respond to the other from a resource available to them both and to *Give Better Back;* that they both know with certainty what will happen if they respond from the protective parts they habitually employ to handle their partner; and that a different, surprising response can open infinite possibilities.

I watched appreciatively as she deftly fielded the automatic objections from their astonished and outraged protective parts, and I could see them both begin to realize that she was guiding them from helplessness to instrumentality. They were learning that they could effectively attend to their own frightened and wounded parts, rather than futilely trying to force the other to change.

They began to see the usefulness of Mona's mantra "If it's intense, it's yours," to realize that each of their intense, overwhelming feelings were signals to look inside rather than to lash out, and that they could each recover access to the parts of themselves that they liked and admired.

I discovered Richard Schwartz's therapy model in June, 1995. I am proud to say that I immediately realized it was a paradigm shift—a conceptual breakthrough that exponentially increased the power of psychotherapy to help and heal. I was forced by this discovery to make the uncomfortable shift from master to student. Happily, my investment of discomfort was fulsomely rewarded, and my study of the IFS model has allowed me an effectiveness and satisfaction I never dreamed my work could provide.

I am also proud to say that I was instrumental in introducing Mona Barbera to the IFS model. She was, at the time, a very talented young therapist who had dedicated herself to healing troubled relationships. She had heard about IFS from a colleague, and because I was then the only IFS therapist in Boston, she came to me to check it out. IFS made the same impression on her that it had on me, and she immediately sought training in the model. I very much enjoyed watching her master IFS, begin in turn to teach it, and now, with this book, to use her brilliance and creativity to make its magic available to couples.

It is a truism that the quality of your relationship with your intimate partner determines the quality of your life more than any other factor. I am therefore confident that the book you hold in your hands has the potential to make a major positive impact on your life. I invite you to join me in thanking Mona Barbera for writing it.

MICHAEL ELKIN

Preface

We fought every day for a year. I had wanted this man from the first time I saw him walk across a room. I married him, we had three great years, and then we could hardly move a desk or have a party without a struggle. Why did such a wonderful partnership have to deteriorate? We sat in a popular couples workshop and learned to take turns listening and speaking, but it didn't help. "It's just words," my husband said. He's not a psychologist—so I thought, "He just doesn't get it."

One day, in the middle of a fight, he just stopped. I kept going, feeling justified, upset, and needing to make him change, but he stayed steady, connected, open, and calm. What was this? If I was doing the usual arguing, defending, threatening, and distancing, why wasn't he?

He started a revolution in our relationship, which I now call "giving better back." It's giving better energy back, with less of the meanness, distance, or insult you feel is coming from your partner. So instead of, "You hurt me—you deserve the same back," it becomes, "You hurt me—I give you better back." I found that giving better back not only helped my marriage, it helped me. Not only was I freeing my husband from having to receive negativity from me, I was freeing myself from having it in myself in the first place. Giving better back became the guiding principle in my life and in my work as a psychologist specializing in couples therapy.

When I look back on it now and realize the immensity of what my husband started, I feel a deep appreciation for his goodness and wisdom.

Then my colleagues persuaded me to take a course in Internal Family Systems[SM] (IFS) from Richard Schwartz. Reluctantly, I drove three hours to a Connecticut classroom, thinking all the way, "I don't need to learn anything new. I'm getting great results in my practice, and I like what I already know." But I listened to Richard explain how we all have different parts within ourselves, how sometimes these parts have to become extreme and take over with their anger, judgment or pain, and how we can stop fighting them and restore our natural state of "Self Leadership." I was stunned. I realized that thinking, "A part of me wants . . . a part of me feels . . ." is not just a figure of speech. It's true—we do have different parts that think, feel, and act in distinctly different and even opposite ways. Sometimes, Richard said, they can get extreme and make us shop too much, be mean to the people we love, or feel immersed in isolation. But we can get to know our parts, hear the stories that have locked them into extreme roles, and free them from isolation and limitation.

Here was a model that recognized how stuck things could get, yet there wasn't a shred of judgment for the most extreme behaviors—only understanding. There was a way to access calm, spacious resources far more powerful than any problem—be it hopelessness, grinding repetition of unproductive behaviors, or the deepest despair. These resources, which Schwartz calls "Self" or "Self energy" (1995, 2001, 2004), have the same limitless and immanent qualities described in religious domains, but there was no bypass or dismissal of psychological problems. I believe that we all have basic goodness, so it was great to know that even my most extreme parts, like the ones that get angry or isolated or feel superior or inferior, are essentially good, too.

Not wanting to give up my seasoned professional identity and become a beginner again, I stalled, asking abstract intellectual questions in the morning session, thinking to myself, "I'm intelligent. I can tell Richard a thing or two." That lasted about an hour (I'm sure Richard and my colleagues were relieved when it was over). After that, I entered the world of IFS and let it enter me, so that now the two don't feel any different. IFS taught me how and why giving better back works, and why it improved my life as well as my relationship.

Now the old, repetitive fights with my husband don't start as often or last as long. I remember a recent one in Costa Rica, the night before I returned to the United States. As we sat in the car with damp bathing suits, looking out at the surf and the sun setting over Playa Hermosa, I suggested that since I had come to Costa Rica six times in the past year to be with him while he looked for a piece of land, would he be willing to do something with me that I liked, that he wouldn't normally want to do, like take a couples workshop back in the States? I'm passionate about my work, and I enjoy the therapy and workshop environment. I wanted the man I love to join me there.

After all, for five days I had lived in his world. I remembered how we had driven up a mountain the day before to meet the brothers who owned it. We saw the four tall "hermanos" coming two by two on horseback over a ridge in the distance. They brought us to the edge of a field overlooking the Pacific and hazy green peninsulas stretching out to the South, and I thought, *this is a great way to get to know the country*. Then they entered a small path into the jungle, stepping over a big pile of fallen branches. Hmm—didn't they say that's where the snakes hide? I had my red rubber boots covering me up to the knees, but the rest of me felt very exposed. The brothers all carried machetes, ready to slice any snake heads that appeared, but they were twenty feet ahead. I found a way around the pile and then willed myself to step over every log on the path, fully expecting to see the gray diamonds of the *terciopele* lunging out from their cool hiding places on the far side. There was a lot of jungle. Then there was a lot of open field, going uphill, under the bright equatorial sun. Nobody was complaining, so I kept quiet and concentrated on putting one foot in front of the other until I made it back to the car and collapsed into the front seat. I just wanted to go to sleep, but I tried to maintain a dignified upright position while my husband

and the four brothers lined up on their haunches in the grass doing business and poking little holes in the ground with their machetes. I was beyond dehydrated—it took a whole day to feel like myself again. Surely, Monk could appreciate how I joined him and would be willing to take one little couples workshop.

Monk said yes, he'd do something with me, anything but a couples workshop. In that instant I started to lose my relaxed playing-on-the-beach feeling. Suddenly, I was twelve years old, sitting at the dinner table with Mom on my left, Dad on my right, and sister Lana directly across. There was a bowl of creamy, homemade tomato soup in front of me, and I wasn't eating it. Mom asked why and I said I didn't like it.

Mom's face seemed to work for a second or two, and then she erupted out of her chair, yelling, "You are an ungrateful, hurtful, hateful child. I can never please you!" and pounded up the stairs to her room. Slam. The three of us sat there in silence, looking away from each other. Dad's eyes were blank and drained, and I knew I wouldn't get a big warm hug that night. We all knew from experience that she wouldn't be down for three days, and it didn't matter if we knocked or pleaded or said we were sorry. She might want to go into the swimming pool in the middle of the night—and she couldn't swim. No one knew what to do. Dad just went to work the next morning.

Many years later, we realized that for my mother, making dinner meant sipping a lot of white wine and vermouth. An ER doctor who was trying to help her sounded impressed when he told us that she could walk and talk normally with a blood alcohol level almost twice the DUI limit! As I sat at that table with my sister and father, I kept very still on the outside so I wouldn't upset anyone anymore. On the inside, a shield was forming around my gut feelings so that I wouldn't know what they were and I wouldn't get hurt from expressing them.

When Monk said, "I don't want to do a couples workshop," he triggered this twelve-year-old part of me. It was as if I were a child back with my family. All I could hear in my head was, "He doesn't ever care about my needs! It doesn't matter what I want." I didn't know this was only part of me because its reality was consuming me. I couldn't notice the hurt twelve-year-old, and I couldn't be there for her.

I didn't show the hurt to Monk. Instead, angry parts leaped out to accuse my husband of not caring and not being fair. And, of course, my angry parts stimulated his angry, attacking parts. Every word out of his mouth sounded as though he was cross-examining a hostile witness.

Several hours later, on a dirt road outside a reggae restaurant, I was finally able to recognize the hurt twelve-year-old within me. I met her where she felt trapped and isolated in that dining room. I felt her relax with my presence and my acknowledgment of her world. I was offering her the Self energy that Richard Schwartz had taught me about. I was doing for her what no one else had done—noticing her pain.

I emerged out of my narrow self-focus and saw Monk standing there in the dark, his shoulders tense and his face blank and hard. He was facing palm trees under the moonlight with the surf crashing fifty feet away, but he wasn't seeing or hearing any of it. He was in pain, too!

I was ready to give better back. I took a deep breath, gave up my angry attitude, and said, "I must have hurt you very much for you to be acting this way." His shoulders dropped and his face softened into its familiar contours. I felt my own tension go away, and I felt a rich, warm, grounded feeling in my center—our connection. I felt our love alive and breathing between us, and I knew I was where I belonged. My twelve-year-old's aloneness was gone, replaced by connection beyond what I ever could have dreamt of as a child.

From this example, you might be thinking that giving better back is all about nurturing and understanding, and not about assertiveness or standing up for your own needs. Giving better back is powerful both when it is compassionate and when it focuses on your needs. We'll learn more about the assertive aspects of giving better back in Chapter 6, *"Giving Better Back,"* and Chapter 10, *"Feedback: The Other Side of the Coin."*

About This Book

This book will show you how to change negative relationship cycles into positive ones so that you can sustain intimacy, creativity, and compassionate connection over time. As you will find out in Chapter 1, you have to turn it upside down—the intense pain you think your partner is causing is really your own. When this pain isn't so intense, you won't have to be immersed in it or so afraid of it that you have to ignore it.

Learning how your protector parts (Managers and Firefighters) work will help you understand what is happening when you and your partner get into cold or fiery standoffs. You'll learn how you can be *with* these important parts instead of *in* them, so that you can access your calm and creativity instead of locking onto limiting beliefs or extreme actions. There will be exercises to help you get to know your own protector parts. Even though you might regret how these parts make you act, you'll find out that they are trying to help you get away from pain inside you.

You will learn that creating lasting change in your relationship depends on finding your own hurt parts. You will have the opportunity to find out what hurts so much that you have to attack or distance from your partner. Once you recognize this pain, as I did when I found my lonely twelve-year-old, you won't be devastated when your partner does something that hurts or disappoints you. You'll be able to experience only moderate hurt and to choose how you want to respond instead of being propelled into anger, blame, or distance.

But it's hard to think clearly when you get tangled up with your partner. Sometimes reactions arise so quickly and powerfully that you can't stop them. If you are in couples therapy, your therapist can help defuse the situation. But at home, it's up to you. Giving better back is a tool that will help you at those times. You will learn how to turn the worst experiences between you and your partner into moments of intimacy, connection, and empowerment, benefitting both you and your relationship.

Choosing a partner is different from maintaining that choice over the years. You will learn that keeping choice alive means meeting the particular challenges that arise in your relationship. As you'll see in Chapter 7, *Keep Choice Alive,* choosing a partner is choosing a specific path of growth for yourself. Meeting the challenges particular to your union will propel your growth in certain directions and not others. In short, who you choose is how you grow.

Have you ever wondered why some people choose safe partners, some choose exciting ones, and some choose partners who offer deep emotional connection? In Chapter 8, *Different Parts Choose Different Partners,* you'll learn how your different parts determine the blend of safety, excitement, and fulfillment in your relationship, and the challenges you face when you make an unbalanced choice.

Some of the biggest problems in couple relationships involve anger, contempt, arguing, distancing, hopelessness, punishing, forcing, and addictions. In Chapter 9, *Caution: Firefighters at Work,* you'll learn that these behaviors are actually attempts to find a solution. Understanding the logic behind these extreme behaviors will help you identify them in yourself and will help you have more compassion when your partner demonstrates them.

Giving feedback to your partner is important. If you hold back your perceptions, your relationship can wither away. In Chapter 10, you'll find out how to give effective feedback, what to expect in response, and how to stay calm, confident, and clear no matter what happens.

Don't worry about getting your partner on board with the ideas in this book. You can do a lot on your own to wake up the love in your relationship. Do your best and see how your partner responds—you might find that your partner responds with more love than you ever thought possible.

I hope that the ideas and the exercises in this book will help you improve your relationship. If you want to seek a couples therapist for additional help, Chapter 13 will tell you what to expect in IFS couples therapy. Both lay people and couple therapists themselves can learn about how couples therapy can be a creative, easy and fluid process.

Some readers may be wondering if all this applies to abusive relationships. Would you still need to recognize your own pain, give better back, choose the challenge, and give feedback if your partner was abusing you or your child, physically or emotionally? If your partner is abusing you or abusing a child, you must consider leaving the relationship, at least temporarily. Once you are safe, you can decide whether to apply the ideas in this book to improve the relationship or leave it.

Acknowledgments

Thanks to Kathrin Seitz, writing coach extraordinaire; all the friends and colleagues who read, listened, and commented; Dick Schwartz for developing and teaching the IFS model; Michael Elkin for his vibrant foreword; all the IFS trainers who have helped me learn the model; the clients who included me in their journeys; and the couples who have allowed me to use their stories in this book.

CHAPTER I

Turn It Upside Down

D o you love your partner but feel hurt or disappointed because of the way he or she acts? Do you think your partner is causing you pain, and all would be well if he would just stop? Do you think you need to pressure, judge, or teach your mate to be different?

If all this effort isn't working out, here's another way to think about your relationship: the intense pain you think your partner is causing is really your own. This topsy-turvy idea will free you from unhappy interactions, release the love you've always wanted, and allow you to give up the project of changing your partner. It focuses your energy where it's needed and most useful: on yourself.

Of course, no one can just passively accept all that their partner does. As the years go by, people know their partners better and better—their unique goodness—but also how they fail themselves and others. Here is the other side of the topsy-turvy manifesto: when you can be calm and connected about your dissatisfaction, it's time to give feedback. When you can express your perceptions without agitation or forcing, and maintain your serenity no matter how your partner responds, you are ready to address conflict in a creative, productive way.

Trying to force your partner to change is not a productive use of your energy and doesn't make love grow. Paying attention to your own intense discomfort so that you can relax is a good use of your energy.

You are capable of making the switch from anger, blame, and distance to loving and connecting—if you are willing to be honest with yourself. When you understand why parts of yourself blame, attack, or distance from your mate and how you can help these parts relax, you have the tools to right yourself when you tilt off center. Immense sources of nourishment and renewal will emerge in your relationship. You will enjoy aliveness that comes from knowing your partner's goodness, even when you feel most triggered by him or her. You will emerge from frustration and the sticky trance of feeling separate and alone, to your natural state of connection and clarity, even when you feel most hurt.

Noticing negative cycles with your partner is the first step to getting out of them. Exercise 1 will help you identify one such cycle. Exercises 2, 3, 4, 5, and 6 in later chapters will build on Exercise 1.

Exercise 1: Identify a Negative Cycle with Your Partner

Think of a negative cycle that keeps happening with your partner. It could be a fight or an interaction that leaves you feeling distant or disconnected. You will see sample responses after each step, drawn from the conflict between my husband and I described in the Preface.

1. What my partner does to start the negative cycle: *he refuses to do something that's important to me.*

    _____
    _____
    _____
    _____
    _____

2. What my partner does or says at the worst moment of the cycle (there could be several "worst moments." Perhaps your partner denies something he or she did, accuses you of something, and then starts to yell. It might be helpful to choose one of the "worst moments" closer to the beginning of the sequence.): *he gets angry when I try to persuade him to do what I want.*

_____
_____
_____
_____
_____
_____

3. My thoughts at the worst point (she never cares about me, she never listens, she never supports me, she's selfish, I don't deserve this, he's always pressuring me): *he doesn't care about what I want. He's selfish. I never get what I need.*

_____
_____
_____
_____
_____
_____

4. My feelings at the worst point (agitation, disconnection, coldness, rage): *anger, agitation.*

_____
_____
_____
_____
_____
_____

5. My words at the worst point: *I do what you want, and you can't do one thing for me. You are so selfish.*

_____

_____

_____

_____

6. My attitude at the worst point: *angry, accusing, blaming, disconnected.*

_____

_____

_____

_____

7. What I do at the worst point: *yell, plead, cry, walk away.*

_____

_____

_____

_____

Was it easy to write what your partner does wrong? It usually is. It's so clear to us when our partners are creating problems. If only they would understand what they are doing and change, things would be so much better. There must be some way to get through to them, even if we have to rage or criticize.

Here's that topsy-turvy idea again: when your partner does his or her worst, focus on yourself, not your partner. Even when you are feeling hurt, demeaned, dismissed, misunderstood, or unappreciated, focus on your own responses and reactions.

You may have lots of objections to that idea. Why me? Isn't responsibility supposed to be a 50/50 deal?

Actually, 100/100 works much better. Here are five reasons to focus entirely on your own response:

1. You are the only one you have control over. You cannot make your partner do anything. Of course you want to, especially if you feel hurt. You may want to command, force, or dominate, all for a good reason. You may get temporary compliance, but it will not last.

2. Forcing your mate will not give you serenity, peace, or confidence. Forcing means overpowering someone, and that means being verbally or physically aggressive. Aggression makes you agitated, not peaceful. You may be temporarily imposing your will, but inside, you will not be relaxed, present, or serene.

3. Even if your mate submits to your will, you won't get love. Submission will be motivated by fear and followed by resentment, distance, and anger. After the temporary high of "victory," you will feel empty.

4. Since you know you forced compliance, you'll always wonder, "Did she really respect/value/understand me, or did she just do it because I made her?"

5. Once a disagreement starts, your partner becomes less receptive than usual. If he is usually reasonable, he will be unreasonable. If she is usually open, she will be defensive. If he usually listens, he will shut you out. You'll learn more about this in Chapter 9, "Caution: Firefighters at Work." Your partner is not him or herself when fighting starts. If you focus on your partner during a fight, you are wasting your efforts. You can't count on your partner to do his or her best in the middle of a fight. Focusing on yourself is much more productive.

Maybe you are thinking, "I'd like to take 100% responsibility for myself, but once I get angry or critical, I can't stop." Or, "I know I'm losing my cool, but I'm just trying to make my point."

Or, "You're right; I need to learn to control myself better. I hate myself when I get that way. "

If so, you are like everyone else. We all get caught up in extreme reactions when we feel hurt by our partners: getting angry, shutting down, giving in, getting frustrated, and judging ourselves and our partners.

There is another way. You can stop your anger and blaming, without forcing, trying to control yourself, or giving up your true feelings. You can focus entirely on yourself, remain calm even when you are very hurt, and get your point across clearly and confidently. You can begin the shift from disconnection to intimacy.

For now, let's learn about how you can get to know what's going on inside you when you are upset with your partner.

CHAPTER 2

I Get Scared When You Take Your Eyes Off the Road

We go from intimacy and happiness to disconnection so quickly. Here's how it happened with Sarah and John:

> My husband and I finally found a day to go hiking, which we love. It was a gorgeous, sunny day and we were almost to the trailhead. My husband kept taking his eyes off the road. I got really angry that he wasn't driving safely, and he thought I was overreacting. I had said this many times before and he never stopped doing it. Once again he wasn't listening to me, and I was angry just when I really wanted to be happy with him.

Sarah couldn't help feeling angry. But she was able to slow down and notice a distinct sequence of experiences within herself. Here is what happened:

> I realized I was having a really angry reaction and I decided to put the focus on my own parts. My parts were convinced it was his fault and at first they didn't want to change. I stayed with them and validated their experience, and asked them to let me know more about why they were so mad.
>
> They showed me scenes of when it was the adults' job to take care of me and they didn't. I almost drowned because adults weren't watching. I was supposed to be protected and my brother abused me.

I thanked them so much for helping and said I'd be back to them another time and they totally trusted me.

I looked up at my husband. "I get scared when you take your eyes off the road. It feels like you aren't taking enough care of me, and it brings back memories for me." It was what I was trying to say when I was angry, but now I could say it straight.

He didn't get angry back! He stopped taking his eyes off the road. He never would have done that in the past because I would have continued to be pissed.

We had a beautiful ride and a great day hiking. I actually felt very cared for, which was what I wanted in the first place when I was getting angry.

When Sarah first got angry about her husband's driving, she was completely focused on his behavior. But she stopped and turned the focus onto herself. She listened inside and heard how convinced she was that it was his fault and that he should change. She called these inner experiences "parts," and said, "I stayed with them and validated their experience, and asked them to let me know more about why they were so mad."

It paid off. She remembered times as a child when she really needed care and protection but didn't get it. Still treating her angry parts with respect, she said, "I thanked them so much for helping and said I'd be back to them another time and they totally trusted me."

Sarah was actually thanking her anger, telling it that it made sense to be angry about being unprotected. She came out of her reverie, spoke to John again about his driving, but in a connected and clear way. Then he freely gave her what she needed.

You may be wondering how Sarah could talk to her anger, get answers back, and have parts trust her.

When you can slow down your angry or defensive responses, you, like Sarah, will find a distinct sequence of experiences within yourself. On the outside, you'll usually find something like anger or judgment. When you keep listening, you'll probably find something softer like fear or loneliness.

Most of the time we act out our anger, attack, distance, agitation, or judgment, without a sense of control or understanding.

When you think of these takeovers as parts with something to say, as Sarah did, and you offer curiosity and respect, you will have a valuable tool to change your bad relationship experiences.

Parts? Talking to Parts?

Treating your experiences as parts of you, and relating directly to them, is immensely helpful. But if you're like Dan, this doesn't make sense. It was more natural for him to talk about his impatience. He could describe how he was always impatient, how his parents were impatient, and how his impatience was acceptable when he was an airplane pilot. But, as his wife, Elizabeth reported, he was still impatient.

When I asked Dan to try an experiment and talk to his impatience, he resisted. I promised that it would be a brief experiment, and we could see how it went afterward.

"Would your impatience let you talk to it?" I asked. To Dan's surprise, the answer was "Yes."

"What do you do for me?" he asked, with genuine curiosity. He heard back, "I demand as little delay as possible, so you don't have to wait. That was useful when you were an airplane pilot."

"But," Dan said, "Waiting is not life threatening now. There is no rush and no emergency in retirement."

Dan looked at me and said, "I'm asking it to retire. It doesn't like it but it's interested in a new direction."

"Why doesn't it like retirement?" I asked.

"It says it has energy, and getting rid of it would be like saying that an integral part of me is no good," Dan replied.

"Ask it what it would like to do with its energy if it didn't have to make you impatient," I suggested.

"Energy," Dan said. "It says it can give me energy for other projects. I need energy to finish my book. I have an enormous need to do things that will help other people and this book would be meaningful to me and others."

It seemed like a cloud crossed Dan's face and I wondered if it was a little wave of grief that he wasn't a pilot anymore. Elizabeth's eyes were glistening and her gaze was soft and connected.

Dan looked like he was satisfied. He had a plan. His impatience was going to transform into energy to finish his book. "How did the experiment go?" I asked. "It was very hard to do," he said, "but I'm not tired. I'm more relieved than tired."

Dan had done the experiment—he talked to his impatience.

Meeting the parts that come up in response to your mate will help you find the most creativity, the greatest resources, the most peace and freedom, and the best solutions for your relationship. Judith Simmer-Brown eloquently describes this process in *Dakini's Warm Breath* (2002, pp. 132-136), her book about the feminine principle in Tibetan Buddhism. She says we all have "wisdom born within," or "experiential wisdom that arises naturally in everyday life." But we don't need to find this wisdom outside of ourselves or try to calm ourselves to evoke it. It is, as Simmer-Brown says,

"inherently present within normal confusion; it is the sanity within neurosis...Often wisdom arises in our experience in the midst of our emotional turmoil."

In order to access this wisdom, she says,

[We must] give up the struggle to reject our suffering and confusion and awaken to the wisdom inherent in our painful experiences...when deep confusion or turmoil arises, with it arises the clarity that can cut through the confusion and turmoil.

When you feel confused, rejected, alone, or angry with your partner, within those very experiences lie vast, spacious, luminous solutions. When you can stop judging your reactions, being immersed in them, or trying to make them go away, you can get to know them. You will find, as Simmer-Brown says, "the inextricability of wisdom and confusion."

Chogyam Trungpa (1988, p.15), a leader in Tibetan Buddhism in America, also describes this kind of awareness and acceptance:

> When you don't punish or condemn yourself, when you relax more and appreciate your mind, you begin to contact the fundamental notion of basic goodness in yourself...We do not have to deceive ourselves or other people...no matter what comes along, we're always standing at the center of the world in the middle of sacred space, and everything that comes into that circle and exists within us there has come to teach us what we need to know.

Martin Smith is an episcopal priest, spiritual director, and retreat leader. In *A Season for the Spirit: Readings for the Days of Lent* (pp. 33-36), he explores the many selves within and how we can be with them.

> As soon as I start a dialogue with myself the reality of self as a kind of society becomes apparent at once... I experience more selves when I become aware of inner conflict around decisions... The Holy Spirit of God dwells in your heart and is no stranger to the diversity and conflict there. The Spirit dwells with and among and between all the selves of your self... There is no secret place where the Spirit has no access, nor any inner person excluded from the Spirit's presence... The Spirit will bring the selves of the self into a unity around the center of the indwelling Christ. The New Self will be a kind of inner community based on the principle of love in which there is room for everyone.

In a meditation, he continues:

> What chance is there of loving and respecting others if I refuse

to meet and listen to the many sides of myself? How can I be a reconciler if I shut my ears to the unreconciled conflicts within myself...Now I begin to see that the spiritual life is based on a basic honesty which enables me to recognize that everything I find difficult to accept, bless, forgive, and appreciate in others is actually present within myself.

CHAPTER 3
Firefighters:
I'm Just Trying to Stop the Pain

Remember Exercise 1, when you wrote what your partner did to make things bad? Did you think you were acting reasonably when your partner attacked, disrespected, or misunderstood you?

That's how we usually feel. The drawings below illustrate the experience of you feeling innocent, under fire from your partner. They come from an animated film I created in 2001. I had written an academic article on conflict in couples relationships (Psychoanalysis and Psychotherapy, 2001), and I wanted to present the ideas in a visual format.

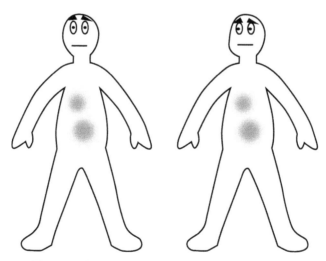

Figure 1. That's you on the left, feeling fine at the moment.

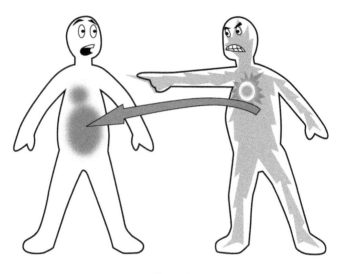

Figure 2

How quickly things change! Your partner has just attacked you. It's possible you did some tiny thing to contribute to the problem, but it probably feels like it's mostly your partner's fault.

You have a couple of little gray blobs inside you. They are your vulnerabilities, your wobbly feelings of fear, sadness, or unworthiness. Before your partner attacked you, you weren't thinking about them. In fact, you rarely think about them. If someone asked you if you were afraid, sad, anxious, or insecure, you'd probably say no. But they are there. In IFS they are called Exiles because we keep them away from our normal awareness.

Exiles are the parts that live silently in old pain, as if it were still happening. They are young children or awkward teenagers, in living rooms or porches or driveways, experiencing confusion, pressure, fear, helplessness, or isolation. They stay in the painful past, never growing up and never realizing that you are an adult and that the pain is behind you. They are the ones who believe, "The past is not dead. In fact, it's not even past" (Faulkner, 1951).

One of your little gray blobs got much bigger in Figure 2. That's because your partner got to it. All of a sudden, the hurt, scared, lonely, unloved feelings you had forgotten are back. You are no longer a capable, secure, reasonable adult—you've swooped back into the past and you are reliving overwhelming feelings. You've lost your calm, confidence, and connection with your partner.

Your partner triggered your Exile, but you probably didn't know it because it was immediately covered up by your Firefighter (Schwartz, 1995, 2001, 2004, 2008).

Figure 3

There's your Firefighter firing back. Just like a real-life Firefighter, it knows there is an emergency and it responds immediately. The emergency is an intense wave of unworthiness, fear, or loneliness, and the mission is to stop it as soon as possible. Since your Firefighter thinks your partner is causing the pain, it attacks him or her.

Notice that the throbbing Exile is gone. What happened? Firefighters rushed out with anger and attack and—no more pain! Anger is the greatest analgesic. Anger comes—pain goes. Criticism, contempt, arguing, distancing, hopelessness, moralizing, lecturing, punishment, and addictions are also pretty good Firefighter tactics. You'll learn about the whole crew in Chapter 9, "Caution: Firefighters at Work."

Since the Firefighters' job description is to stop your pain immediately, they don't care about being nice. They will force, shame, blame, or punish with impunity. Of course, your partner is likely to attack back.

Understanding Firefighters will make a huge difference in your relationship. They are the parts of you that cause you and your partner to rage at each other or stomp away into lonely, stony distance.

Identifying Firefighters

The purpose of Firefighters is to stop pain as quickly as possible. In order to do their jobs, Firefighters need to eliminate caring or concern for others and focus on getting the job done ASAP. Therefore, a Firefighter will have some or all of the following characteristics:

> Doesn't care about your partner's feelings
> Agitated
> Disconnected
> Blaming or shaming
> Forcing

Exercise 2: Identifying Firefighters

Look back at what you wrote in Exercise 1, Questions 3-7. Check off the statements that apply to your responses.

> ____ I don't care about my partner's feelings.
> ____ I am agitated rather than calm.
> ____ I feel disconnected from my partner.
> ____ I am blaming or shaming my partner.
> ____ I am trying to force my partner to do something.

If you've checked even one statement, your response could be a Firefighter taking over. Perhaps when you see what you've checked, you will not be proud of your actions. Write your self-criticisms here:

_____

_____

_____

_____

_____

Now remind yourself that your Firefighter is only trying to protect you. As long as Exiles are in pain, Firefighters have a job to do. They believe you are at risk from what your partner just did. They vividly remember times when you were smaller, younger, severely stressed, or defenseless. They confuse the past with the present and conclude that you need emergency protection.

Can you acknowledge your Firefighter for its efforts? Even though Firefighters cause damage in relationships, and you criticize yourself for your Firefighter-driven behavior, their efforts are often skillful, immediate, energetic, and designed to help.

In the following exercise, you will have the opportunity to understand and acknowledge your Firefighter. You will find that this approach gives you better results than judging or resisting your Firefighter.

Exercise 3: Getting to Know Your Firefighter

Look at what you wrote in Exercise 2. Think of yourself being uncaring, agitated, disconnected, blaming, shaming, or forcing. That is your Firefighter trying to help you. If you find yourself judging your Firefighter, gently ask the judgment to step aside.

1. What does your Firefighter look like? See if you can be open to new perceptions. Perhaps you'll see a person, an animal, a shape, or a color.

    _____

    _____

    _____

    _____

2. What is it doing?

    _____

    _____

    _____

    _____

    _____

3. How is your Firefighter responding to you? Is it aware that you are paying attention to it? If it is ignoring you, ask it why. Listen to its answer. It might be so used to being judged that your curiosity is disconcerting. See if you can interact with it so that it relaxes and senses your genuine interest.

    _____

    _____

    _____

    _____

4. Ask your Firefighter if it wants you to know anything about it. Does it want you to understand how it serves you? What does it do well? Why does it think you need it? Does it think you lack abilities to handle the situation with your partner?

    _____

    _____

    _____

    _____

5. Ask your Firefighter what bad thing would happen if it stopped doing what it usually does.

    _____

    _____

    _____

    _____

    _____

6. How do you feel toward your Firefighter now? If there is any judgment or rejection, gently ask it to step aside. If it won't, listen to the judgment and see if it calms down. If the judgment persists, be patient. Just let it be, and try to finish this exercise another time.

_____

_____

_____

_____

7. What happens when you dialogue with your Firefighter? Can you acknowledge it and offer understanding? How does it respond?

_____

_____

_____

_____

8. Ask your Firefighter if it will step back and allow you to handle the situation with your partner at the worst moment in the cycle. Does it need any reassurance from you that you can do this well?

_____

_____

_____

_____

9. What is it like to be friendly and curious toward your Firefighter?

_____

_____

_____

_____

_____

Getting to Know Your Firefighter Is a Relief

If you were able to be curious and respectful toward your Firefighter, you probably feel relieved. You may feel a new sense of integration and wholeness. Perhaps you discovered that accepting your Firefighter is much more effective than judging it, or maybe you found out that your Firefighter is weary from so much emergency duty.

When you understand Firefighters, you understand that the worst, most hurtful behaviors in relationships come from Firefighters who have good intentions; they want to make the pain go away. Most of the cycles of disconnection, blame, anger, and forcing in relationships are the exchanges of Firefighters.

As long as you have Exile pain, your Firefighters have to work to protect you.

When your partner breaches the perimeter protecting your Exiles, Firefighters leap in to snuff out the pain. They don't stop to think—they just attack, force, distance, or disconnect. Firefighters act to stop the hurt.

You will learn more about Firefighters in Chapter 9. For now, it is important to remember that Firefighters will keep doing their jobs as long as you have Exile pain within you. If Firefighters didn't have Exiles to protect, they wouldn't have to work so hard. But what can you do in couple relationships when you feel the intense reactions of Firefighters taking over? How can you avoid fueling the toxic cycles of Firefighters?

CHAPTER 4

If It's Intense, It's Your Own

When you feel intense hurt in your relationship, it's easy to think that your partner is causing it. He or she does or says something and you immediately feel hurt. It's obvious that his or her actions are the problem. Your partner should change so you can feel better.

But the truth about the pain is just the opposite. As I like to tell my clients, "If it's intense, it's your own." When hurt fills your entire being, and you can't even remember feeling safe and capable, you are experiencing the hurt of your Exiles. Blaming or distancing from your partner doesn't take the pain away. Your Exiles will still hurt inside, and you'll also have to deal with a partner who is angry about being attacked or abandoned.

Most people vacillate between too much awareness of Exiles' feelings and none at all. It's as if there were a switch instead of a thermostat for the heat in a house, and it can only be totally off or blasting full force. There's no opportunity to adjust the dial for moderate, comfortable levels of heat. It's hard to get to know your Exiles when you are either completely unaware of them or totally consumed by them. Let's see how Edward found a way to slow the process down and get to know his young, hurt Exile.

Edward Finds His Exile

Edward and Janice were in their fifties when they came for couples therapy. They had been married for 25 years, raised a son and a daughter, and achieved success in their careers. They had a vacation home in New Mexico, friends, and financial ease—but something was missing.

As they sat in my office on their first visit, I found myself interested in Edward's creative way of speaking and Janice's soft presence. But it soon became clear that Edward was very disturbed with the marriage. "I feel a distance between us," he said to Janice. He looked straight at her and continued, "I don't know how long I can go on like this. You reject my ideas. I don't think you love me." Janice's whole body flinched and tears collected in the corners of her eyes. "How could you think I don't love you?" she asked.

Janice sat quietly with her eyes locked onto Edward, letting him lead the session. I asked her what she was thinking, and she said to Edward, "When you get agitated, I shut off. I get paralyzed. I just say nothing because nothing works."

Edward accepted my invitation to look at his side of the problem. In the next few sessions, he talked about "a big lid" he had inside him, covering issues so dark and intense that he could never see them, much less resolve them. Whenever Janice questioned his judgment, the lid came off and he erupted with "insane fury" until she collapsed into tears. Then he had to wait days for Janice to want to be close again, "wallowing" in his loneliness, repeating "poor me" to himself, and kicking himself for being weak and self-indulgent. He was beginning to think that he contributed to the distance between himself and Janice.

But what was under the lid? Edward described his childhood.

> My father was very angry. He locked himself in the bathroom with
> a can of gasoline when I got engaged to Janice because she wasn't
> Jewish. When my son was born and we didn't circumcise him, he

sent me hate letters for two weeks. When I was five, I would knock my head against the wall because I was so frustrated with my father's anger. My mother would watch and say, "Oh look, there he goes again. See how stupid he is."

The content of Edward's stories was disturbing, but his expression as he told them was the same as when he talked about going on a business trip and leaving his computer charger at home. Explaining and analyzing his father's anger didn't change his behavior or relieve him of the heaviness within. Edward didn't have a personal connection with the parts that were under the lid.

After six sessions, Edward and Janice told me they were fighting less and feeling more connected with each other. But when I asked Edward how much of the problem remained, he answered, "Seventy-five percent."

We had to get under the lid to make any significant progress. The image of the boy banging his head on the wall while his mother mocked him was so vivid to me. "Is that boy with you now?" I asked Edward. "Yes," he said. He started to analyze again, explaining what he knew about his father's anger and his mother's mocking. I asked, "Would the analyzer be willing to step aside so we can get to know the boy?"

Edward's thoughtful expression changed to surprise, but he knew that analyzing wasn't getting him anywhere. "But I don't want to wallow in those feelings. What good would that do?"

"Would the part that is worried about wallowing be willing to step aside so you can be with the boy?" I asked. "Okay, but what will happen then?" Edward asked. We were all silent for a few moments, and it seemed as though nothing was happening. Then Edward's voice softened and he said, "I'm there with him. He's facing away from me. We're in a dark corner. He knows I'm there. I'm hugging him from the back."

Janice and I both sat up straight and paid close attention because we knew that Edward wasn't talking about the boy—he was there with him, engaged in a real-time conversation with him.

Janice's face was soft, and her eyes were bright with tears. In the following dialogue, Edward shows us what it's like to talk to one of your parts.

> Mona: What's happening now?
>
> Edward: He can turn away from my mother because I'm there. He didn't know he could do that.
>
> Mona: How is that for him?
>
> Edward: He's intensely grateful. He didn't know he could turn away from my mother. Now he isn't alone and he doesn't have to keep banging his head against the wall. I didn't know how badly he needed that hug. I'm wrapped up in peace and calm now.

The air in my office felt fluid and alive. The silence felt spacious. We all knew something big had happened. Edward said, "I never thought I could reach in and be the support for that little boy, the support he never had back then. That's the magic. I never knew it could happen, even when you were guiding me through it. I didn't know it could happen and then it just did."

Edward's Exile was the boy who was hurt by his father's anger and devastated by his mother's mocking. Even though these actual events were in the past, within Edward they were as vivid and painful as the day they happened. The boy who had banged his head on the wall in a corner was still doing it, alone and helpless.

Edward couldn't connect with his Exile through analyzing his past. Simply understanding what had happened didn't change anything. He had to let go of analyzing and wait to see what would happen.

In Exercise 4, you will have the opportunity to find an Exile within yourself. Referring back to Exercise 2, "Identifying Firefighters," the first question you will answer is, "What painful feeling did you have just before you lost your caring, calm, or connection, or when you started to blame, shame, or force?"

That is not such an easy question to answer. Neither are the following ones that ask you to look at and listen to your Exile. That's because you have a system inside you designed to keep Exiles out.

Human exiles in the real world are banished beyond the borders of their countries. They are not welcome, they cannot reenter, and/or it is unsafe for them to enter. Immigration officials guard the perimeters of countries day and night, letting cars or people in one at time, checking to be sure the unwanted don't get in.

It's the same with Exiles within you. "Managers" are the parts that act like immigration officials within you, keeping Exiles out so you won't feel their despair, depression, fear, or loneliness. Managers are organized, persistent, and effective.

Once you begin Exercise 4, your Managers will start working. They will see that you are trying to bring an Exile into your consciousness and say, "No, we can't let him in. You can't have that person come inside the boundaries. The decision has already been made and it's in your best interest."

If you ask Question 1, and stay aware of your thoughts, you might hear reasonable, reflective, intelligent statements such as the following:

> "True, I did lose my connection and caring. But that's because I felt overpowered. I've had that problem all my life, and it's because my father/mother/older sibling didn't respect me."
>
> "Yes, I did start forcing my partner to see my point of view. But that's because I never felt loved in my family, and it felt like he/she didn't care about me enough."

Those are all valid statements of self-awareness. But they are analyzing your responses. That is Manager behavior, and it will prevent actual contact between you and your Exiles. That's what Edward wanted to do.

Or you might be aware of some of your Exile's feelings—fear, fuzziness, or shame— within you, but in a muted and distant way.

That's also the work of Managers. They can let you know you have a feeling, but they keep it controlled.

Analyzing and controlling are typical Manager activities. When you look for your Exile, you will probably start analyzing or get only a vague sense of the fear or unworthiness in your Exile. You will have a sincere intention to find your Exile and connect with it directly, but it probably won't happen right away.

That's why, in Questions 2 and 3, you will be talking to your Managers. You will acknowledge their fears and concerns and reassure them that you can handle your Exile. Managers are good parts and they want the best for you. If they can be persuaded that you are an adult and that you have more resources and resilience than you had as a child, and that meeting your Exile will be beneficial, they will probably be willing to give you a chance.

You'll be checking in with your Managers at the end of the exercise. Question 6 tells you to "Go back to the Managers you found in Questions 2 and 3. Ask them what they think about what happened in this exercise." You will find that your Managers probably liked what happened. If you keep listening, you'll hear that they actually don't like their jobs much. They are often tired, grim, and limited. They direct all their thoughts, actions, and creativity to one goal: making sure old pain is not triggered. They keep a constant watch, limiting daily life and potential for intimacy so that Exiles aren't triggered. If they could trust you enough to relax and let you handle things, life would be a lot better for them.

Now you will have the opportunity to find an Exile within yourself. You can use the negative cycle you described in Exercise 1 as a starting point, or you can do Exercise 1 over again and use a different negative cycle.

This exercise will help you approach your Exile with curiosity and compassion so that it will open up to you and show you its pain. You may find that you're not just thinking about it but also being with it in the present.

Exercise 4: What Is Your Firefighter Protecting?

Go back to Exercise 2 and look at what you checked off. Picture the disagreement between you and your mate, see yourself responding, and notice how it makes your body feel. Answer the following questions.

1. What painful feeling(s) did you have just before you lost your caring, calm, and connection and started to disconnect, blame, shame, or force? Did you feel alone, betrayed, abandoned, unlovable, invisible, helpless, or cornered?

    _____
    _____
    _____
    _____
    _____
    _____
    _____

2. Do you want to avoid these painful feelings? Why? Are you afraid they won't go away, concerned that they will overwhelm you or that they will make you feel weak or look crazy to others? Or are you starting to analyze your responses? You are probably encountering your Managers. Listen to them with respect and patience.

    _____
    _____
    _____
    _____
    _____

3. What can you say to reassure your Managers that it's okay to notice these feelings? For instance, "I'll take it a step at a time," "These feelings come from an Exile that needs acknowledgment," "It doesn't work to keep avoiding it," "I'll just try this and see how it works." You can even tell your Managers they can jump in and intervene if they think something dangerous is happening.

_____

_____

_____

_____

4. Look for the painful feeling inside you. Does it look like a person? Do you feel it as a sensation inside or around your body? Sometimes it's easier to think of it as a person so the following questions use the pronouns he or she. If the pronouns are distracting to you, just ignore them and answer intuitively.

_____

_____

_____

_____

_____

Where is he or she?

_____

_____

_____

_____

_____

What is he or she doing?

_____

_____

_____

_____

Does he or she want to say anything to you or show you anything?

_____
_____
_____
_____

Now that you have found your Exile, see if you can be accepting and curious. Can your Exile feel the comfort of knowing you are there? Respect you Exile's pace. It may need more time to develop trust.

5. Ask your Exile if he or she wants anything from you. Does he or she want you to listen, give him or her a hug, or take him or her somewhere else? You can ask this question out loud, or just imagine you are asking it.

_____
_____
_____
_____

6. Go back to the Managers you found in Questions 2 and 3. Ask them what they think about what happened.

_____
_____
_____

Exiles want you to notice and understand them. That might seem inconsequential to you, but it means so much to Exiles. When Exiles feel the comfort and safety of your presence, they relax. They are children who need attention and safety, and when they get it, they want to let go of their pain.

If you are like most people, you usually ignore your Exiles, relieved that they, and their grim experiences, are out of your awareness. You judge them as weak, crazy, or dangerous. Or, if they can break through the barriers imposed upon them, they flood you with their sad, scared, or angry feelings, just as a wave crashes over you in the surf. Then you hate them even more, resenting how they disrupt your life and make you feel scared or helpless again.

If you take the time to find and acknowledge your Exiles, they won't flood you as much when your partner does something that hurts you. They might still feel sad, scared, or angry when your partner does things that remind them of their sad pasts, but only moderately so. As your Exiles soften over time, you will be watching the wave as it rolls in from the ocean, feeling calmer as you remember old pain.

Now that you have found an Exile that gets triggered in the negative cycle with your partner, can you imagine being at the worst point in that cycle and having a moment to make a choice before you react? What might your choice be? Answer the following questions.

1. If you didn't have to feel such intense pain at the worst point in the negative cycle with your partner, what would you like to do differently?

    _____

    _____

    _____

    _____

    _____

2. How would you feel about yourself if you did this?

    _____

    _____

    _____

    _____

    _____

3. What effect do you think it might have on the negative cycle?

    _____

    _____

    _____

    _____

    _____

Noticing and befriending your Exiles is the most powerful thing you can do to stop negative cycles in your relationship. When you do this, you will be able to accept yourself as you are, and your Exiles won't have to flood you with painful feelings. You won't have a shocked feeling when your partner does something hurtful in a negative cycle, and you won't have to attack or distance. You will have a moment of calm to choose what you want to do and will find yourself making clear, calm, connected responses you could never have imagined before. Spontaneous, unforeseen, surprising creativity will arise, profoundly altering the dull repetition of negative cycles. An upward spiral of generosity, connection, and compassion will replace the downward spiral of criticism, contempt, and distance. Your love will not depend on good circumstances or good behavior from your partner. As the years go by, you can look back and know you gave your best, even when it was challenging.

You may be wondering what it really means to find a part and get to know it. Let's learn more about you and your parts in relationship.

CHAPTER 5

You and Your Parts in Relationship

We've been talking about "parts" within you since page one. Maybe it has felt natural to you. Or maybe it seems strange to think of yourself as having parts. Many people feel that way at first. But they usually discover that they can solve their relationship problems by focusing on parts, unblending from them, listening to them, and understanding if and why they have become extreme.

Blending and Unblending

Focusing on your parts brings relief and opens you up to creative possibilities. But you cannot focus on a part while it is consuming you with its reality. You can focus on your parts if you are aware of them, but not immersed in them (Schwartz, 1997, 2001, 2004, 2008).

It's best to be "unblended" from a part. That means having the part's feelings and beliefs, and being calm, connected, and rational at the same time. When you unblend, you can hear your part saying, "I have to be angry to get my point across, I have to disconnect to be safe, I am helpless, I am alone, I am worthless, I don't matter," without succumbing to its feelings and beliefs. You can watch your part, as you would watch a big wave from the safety of the beach, instead of being in the water and having it crash on your head and throw you to the bottom. You can feel your part physically, as a sensation in or around you, and still feel your feet on the ground, the air on your skin, and the beating in your heart.

Often, the turning point in a negative couple cycle comes when you unblend. You don't have to change the way you feel— just notice the feeling instead of being immersed in it. Sometimes doing this out loud makes a big difference. Just saying to your partner, "I know I'm being defensive (or unreasonable, distant, argumentative) is enough to relieve tension. Maybe you will find yourself laughing with your partner instead of enduring hours of arguing or stony silence. You'll get a chance to practice this in Exercise 5, below.

Exercise 5: Unblending

Look back at Exercise 1, where you described a negative cycle with your partner and your response at the worst moment. Starting with Question 3, "My thoughts at the worst point," Copy your answers below, adding any new details you can remember.

My thoughts at the worst point:

_____
_____
_____
_____
_____
_____
_____
_____
_____
_____
_____
_____

My words at the worst point:

_____
_____
_____
_____
_____
_____
_____
_____
_____
_____

My attitude at the worst point:

_____
_____
_____
_____
_____
_____
_____
_____
_____
_____

What I do at the worst point:

_____
_____
_____
_____
_____
_____
_____

Now answer these additional questions:

1. Picturing yourself in the negative cycle, notice how you feel (sad, tense, relaxed, confused, shocked, isolated, angry, hopeless, frustrated, calm, or judgmental).

    _____
    _____
    _____

2. What do you look like when you respond at the worst moment? Can you see your face, eyes, posture, or the way you are moving? Do you look different from usual? Are you leaning forward, speaking loudly, pointing, attacking, looking helpless, or staring ahead? Write your observations here.

    _____
    _____
    _____

3. Take a moment to go inside, turning your eyes and awareness from the outside to the inside. Just notice—don't try to change a thing. Do you see a part of you inside acting a particular way at the worst moment in your negative cycle? Does your body feel a certain way? Is there a particular statement you are making to yourself? We are going to refer to this experience as a "part" from now on. Write your observations below.

    _____
    _____
    _____

4. Is your part intensely angry or upset? If it is, ask it to tone it down a little so you can be with it. What happens?

    _____
    _____
    _____

5. Ask the part you are noticing to step off to the side—not to go away, but just to separate from you so you can notice it. Write below what happens when you make this request.

    _____

    _____

    _____

    _____

    _____

6. If you have a sense of separation or unblending, skip to Question 9. Often, parts won't step aside when you first ask. They often think you are being antagonistic toward them. Below, write any antagonistic or negative thoughts you have toward this part (you're too angry, you're too passive, you're too needy, you're too intense, I wish you would go away).

    _____

    _____

    _____

    _____

    _____

7. See if you can let go of these antagonistic and negative thoughts for now. You probably won't be able to unblend from a part if you are judging it. Write what happens when you try to let go of your negative feelings. If the antagonistic or negative part won't step back, ask it why. Maybe it doesn't know how. Or does it believe you won't pay attention to it if it steps aside? Is it afraid something bad will happen if it steps aside? Write its reasons below.

    _____

    _____

    _____

    _____

    _____

8. Go back to the part you were focusing on in Step 5. Ask it to step aside again. If it won't, ask it why. Maybe it doesn't know how. Or does it believe you won't pay attention to it if it steps aside? Is it afraid something bad will happen if it steps aside? Write its reasons below.

_____

_____

_____

_____

9. Respond to your part's concern (I will give you better attention if you step aside, I want to listen to you, just try to separate, I won't let anything bad happen). What happens?

_____

_____

_____

_____

10. If your part can separate a little, notice how you feel. Do you feel a sense of spaciousness? Does your body feel different? Are you feeling curious, accepting, or compassionate toward your part? If there is any judgment, see if you can let it go.

_____

_____

_____

_____

11. Thank your part for trusting you.

Talking to Parts vs. Talking about Them

As you may have noticed in the preceding exercise, when parts unblend, you can talk to them. You can have feelings toward them, as you would with anyone you talk to, and your feelings can change as the conversation progresses. Think of someone you were recently talking to. Did you feel close, distant, judgmental, or curious toward him or her? It's the same with parts.

If you think about it, you'll realize that you already talk to your parts. Do you ever hear yourself thinking:

> Just go along with what he or she wants. But I have needs, too. But conflict scares me. I'm angry! But I can't be angry because people won't like it.

Inner dialogues like this are your parts expressing their different points of view. They are talking among themselves without the benefit of your presence.

When partners arrive for their first session of couples therapy with me, they often want to explain why they have a feeling. "I only talked on the phone for ten minutes and he got angry. I feel so hurt because he never listens." When I ask if they would like to get to know the hurt part, they don't know what that means. They want to keep explaining why they felt hurt.

When clients actually do get to know their parts, it can be startling at first. It can feel like a giant, scary leap to be with parts instead of talking about them. Clients often ask, "What if my part answers me—does that mean I'm crazy?"

No, it doesn't. When you talk to your parts and hear them answer, it means you are present to the reality within you. The weird feeling passes, leaving a natural sense of relatedness and creativity. New solutions to your problems will emerge, and you'll be free from repetitive conflicts.

Once you succeed in being with your parts and talking to them, you won't want to go back to the old ways. You will feel cheated unless you ask your parts what they think instead of assuming you know.

Analyzer Parts

If you decide to go on the adventure of getting to know your parts, you are likely to meet analyzer parts. Have you ever found yourself in a conversation with your partner, explaining why you are angry or offering a counterpoint to everything he or she says?

What a surprise it is to find out that this analyzing activity is just a part! Maybe you thought this was just being rational, that it would help bring clarity, or that it was the best way to get your point of view across.

Analyzer parts try to help by explaining and describing. They think it will help you if they organize and reproduce the knowledge you already have.

Someone once described analyzer activity as "rearranging glass figurines on a shelf." You can move them around, but you really don't get a major new look if you're working with the same glass figurines on the same shelf.

When you get to know your analyzers, you'll find that they are proud of their observations and conclusions but tired of working hard without getting results. They don't know that you can connect directly with your other parts, and that those parts will relax in the warmth of your connection, understanding, and acknowledgment.

Analyzer parts will be glad to know that there is a better way and happy for an opportunity to relax. They will find that letting you speak directly to your other parts is far superior to talking about them.

Being curious towards your parts is better than analyzing them and telling them why they are the way they are. When you move away from analyzing your different emotions and reactions to viewing them as parts needing acknowledgement and appreciation, you will have access to more resources, calm, and intelligence than ever before.

A curious attitude works well with your partner, far better than analyzing and telling them why they are the way they are. More importantly, it works well within you. When you move away from analyzing your different emotions and reactions, to viewing them as parts needing acknowledgement and appreciation, you will have access to more resources, calm, and intelligence than ever before.

All Parts Are Good

Once you get beyond your analyzer parts, you'll find your Exiles, the hurt parts stowed away in the background. They need your attention and they need relief, but often the first response they get is judgment.

These hurt parts, isolated in the dark, can seem unappealing at first. Their feelings—neediness, fear, abandonment, or unworthiness—can be threatening. You might want to recoil, and you might even feel disgust. Maybe you think that your success in life depends on keeping Exiles far away, or that people won't like you if they knew what was inside you.

Despite your initial reaction, you will find that all parts are good. No parts are intrinsically bad. No matter how bad they look or feel at first, they are good at heart. When you approach your parts with acceptance and curiosity, their goodness, vulnerability, and richness will always touch you.

When you are respectful and open to parts, you will find that even behaviors like raging, passivity, or paralyzing confusion are not innate character flaws, but instead behaviors that exist within a context. If you listen well enough, you will understand what drives parts to their extreme behaviors. When you believe that all parts are good and you offer curiosity to all that lies within you, you will not have to fight yourself or try to change yourself. You will be able to rest in the natural flow of who you are, knowing that all that arises in you is there for a good reason.

Parts Become Extreme

If all parts are good, why do anger, neediness, fear, isolation, or addictions cause so much trouble? How can these things be good when they cause so much pain in relationships?

Extreme behaviors come from parts trying to adapt to difficult experiences. Perhaps you felt abandoned, ignored, or afraid when you were young and/or helpless. This kind of pain doesn't melt away into the past. It keeps hurting. In order to pay attention at school or have fun with your friends, you have to find a way to lock it away. Exiles do that for you, keeping the unresolved pain far away from consciousness.

Once the pain is locked away in an Exile, Managers and Firefighters make sure it stays there. They make sure you don't trust too much or that you don't let people get close enough to know the truth. When parts have to be so vigilant, they lose their naturally fluid state. They have to stay in narrow roles, focusing on what they *have* to do rather than what they *want* to do. They are constantly active, repelling what they think is bad or holding onto what they think is good. There is no rest or serenity—only constant movement between extremes. There is little opportunity for rest or spontaneity.

Parts Are Waiting to Be Relieved of the Need to Be Extreme

Even though parts get locked into extreme roles and resist change, they wish they could relax. Parts find comfort in doing the familiar, even if it's stressful, but they prefer not to have to do it. When you ask a part, "Would you like it if you didn't have to feel or act that way?" it eventually says, "Yes." Like people, parts enjoy variety and options rather than staying locked into narrow, fear-based roles.

What Is a Part?

Are you wondering what a part actually is? If you experience your parts, unblend from them, and relate to them with curiosity and compassion, it may not be important to you to define them. However, if you want to know how others understand parts, let's start with Richard Schwartz, the founder of the Internal Family

Systems model. He writes (1995),

> ... these internal entities are more than clusters of thoughts or feelings, or mere states of mind. Instead, they are seen as distinct personalities, each with a full range of emotion and desire, and of different ages, temperaments, talents, and even genders. These inner people have a large degree of autonomy, in the sense that they think, say, and feel things independent of the person within whom they exist ... the inhabitants of our internal systems respond best to ... respect, so it is best to treat them that way—to attribute to them human qualities and responses.

Continuing his description of parts in his 2004 article, "The Larger Self," he says:

> Even the worst impulses and feelings—the urge to drink, the compulsion to cut oneself, the paranoid suspicions, the murderous fantasies—spring from parts of a person that themselves have a story to tell and the capacity to become something positive and helpful to the client's life. The point of therapy isn't to get rid of anything, but to help it transform.

Even though Buddhist teachers don't talk about parts in the way that IFS does, their concepts are relevant. Buddhists believe that we all have the innate capacity to meet all life experiences with acceptance and openness (Chodrun, 1991, p. 72-73), and that people are happiest when they can accept change instead of fighting it.

Parts in their natural, unburdened state experience this same openness. When parts don't have to take on protective duties or interpret situations according to the past, they open to situations as they arise. They can live in a world of impermanence and change, adapting to the moment, enjoying what they have, and letting go of what they lose.

When parts are burdened with pain, they have to worry about losing the little worthiness, security, or control that they have. They stay busy protecting themselves or trying to manage pain, and they can't be fully open to what is happening around them. They lock into rock-solid, un-changing ways of thinking about themselves and life—"I'm not worthy, people are scary, I can't control my world." They think they are permanently abandoned, permanently hurt, or permanently afraid. Even if the disturbing events that engendered these beliefs happened in the past, burdened parts experience them as if they are permanently happening and permanently true.

When parts are unburdened, they don't have to think about themselves in any particular way. They are freed from repetitive, permanent thoughts of danger and unworthiness. Instead of solid, unchanging beliefs, they are free to think one thing one moment and another the next.

You may wonder if it is possible for you to feel free of your burdens. You are so accustomed to them, you may not be able to imagine them gone. Or maybe you've tried so many times to get rid of your burdens, that you have lost hope. You are so good at managing with your burdens there that the thoughts of not having them might even be disorienting.

According to the IFS model, you can be free of your burdens. Not the memories, but the sense of imprisonment and pain, and also the need to protect. When you achieve this, you don't have to get angry at your partner when they touch a sore spot. You can remain curious and calm, and have a surprisingly fresh interchange.

In the IFS model, the agent of unburdening is within you. It's called Self.

Self Energy

Self or Self Energy is a presence within or around you with the following qualities (Schwartz, 1995, 2001, 2004):

Curiosity
Calm
Compassion
Confidence

Courage
Clarity
Connectedness
Creativity

Self energy is always available. No matter how hurt you have been or how protective you have become, Self is never diminished. Access to Self may be blocked, but it is always there. Regardless of the severity of your problems, you still have access to boundless qualities of Self.

Self qualities arise spontaneously when extreme emotions don't obscure them. You don't have to do anything to create them. You don't have to develop Self qualities because they are already in you.

Self energy is available to you, even at the worst moments in your negative relationship cycles. You can direct it toward your own parts, or toward your partner, no matter what he or she is doing. Every day I see couples find relief and connection by unblending and accessing Self energy. I still vividly remember the first time I saw Self energy emerge, many years ago, in a demonstration session led by Richard Schwartz. In the afternoon of my first IFS training day, Richard announced that he was going to do a demonstration session. Who wanted to be the client? Hands went up around the room even though no one knew what to expect. Everyone chose a number from one to ten, and Richard chose Albert when he got closest to the right number. He and Richard moved their chairs into the middle of the room. The rest of us took up spots around them in chairs and on the floor.

Richard asked Albert what he wanted to work on, and he responded that he had a problem with shame. "Do you have any concerns about working on shame in front of the group?" Richard asked. Albert was afraid of exposure to the group, that nothing would happen, and that maybe it would be more than he could handle. With each response, Richard asked if that part would step aside so Albert could get to know his shame. When a part wouldn't step aside, Richard asked, "How do you feel toward the part? How far away is it? What does it want you to know?" I was surprised that Richard was calling these concerns "parts," but it didn't seem to faze Albert. He answered quietly, his eyes focused inward.

Richard wasn't asking the usual therapy questions—how long Albert had felt shame, what had made it worse recently, or who in his childhood had shamed him. He focused only on Albert's moment-to-moment experience, with no persuading, judging, or analyzing. I didn't know it at the time, but Richard was helping Albert unblend.

The process was powerful, but not in a tricky or manipulative way. It was flowing as naturally as the earth turns, a flower unfolds, or the wind blows. I could feel it healing me as it healed Albert. As the session progressed, my breathing evened out and my face, usually automatically smiling, relaxed into its own contours. I felt as though I had come home.

The process kept going deeper. When they got to the shame, Albert saw an eight-year-old boy within him who was still hearing the taunts of his alcoholic father. "Fight for yourself! Don't be a wimp!" the boy heard as his father towered over him. Albert was listening to the experiences of this boy with complete presence and compassion and with no desire to change him or judge him. His face crumpled as he witnessed the experience of the young boy within him. But it wasn't consuming him. Tears flowed freely down his cheeks, as if they were washing his burdens away. I was amazed that I hadn't paid much attention to him before, thinking that he was just an ordinary nice guy. How could I not have seen this glorious openness?

At the end of the process, when Albert's eyes rose and scanned the faces around the room, people beamed back at him with gratitude and joy. He was relaxed and confident, accepting people's thanks and appreciation. The process had released him from the burdens of shame.

I didn't know that much about it at the time, but Albert was relating to his hurt eight-year-old with Self energy—with the qualities listed above: curiosity, calm, compassion, confidence, courage, clarity, connectedness, and creativity.

Self Energy Has No Agenda

Did you notice in the example above that Richard Schwartz wasn't funneling Albert in any particular direction or expecting him to respond in a particular way? Even when he asked if Albert's parts would step aside, it was fine if they didn't. Richard was just curious about why. There was no agenda and no pressure to do anything.

So often, when we lack Self energy, we think we know what needs to happen, and we devote our energy to trying to change ourselves or other people. But paradoxically, people—and parts—change more readily when they don't feel forced.

Instead of having an agenda or pushing parts in a particular direction, Self energy is attentive and curious. Questions come out of a desire to understand, not a desire to push or fix. Self invites parts to reveal themselves with the rhythm that feels right to them, and follows them as they zigzag through their beliefs, feelings, and experiences.

It can be a giant leap of faith to stop pushing and start listening to parts, but you will always find that parts have something to say, and that they will respond in ways that enrich your life.

Self Is Compassionate

Self is compassionate. Even when your partner is raging, attacking, or distancing, you can maintain compassion and avoid judgment or distancing. You can stay connected and open your heart to your partner's painful experience. Your compassion will touch your partner and invite him or her to reveal the reasons for their actions. You'll find out that your partner's hurtful behavior was an attempt at self-protection, driven by the beliefs of hurt Exiles and their protectors.

You can offer compassion to your own parts as well. They will open up to you and reveal the contexts that drive them to their extreme behavior. Compassion toward your parts is much more effective than judging them.

Self Is Creative

Self is creative. Once your parts step aside and allow Self energy to appear, you will find solutions that you could never have imagined before. You and your partner will find your way out of problems in brilliant, surprising ways. With Self energy, you will find immense benefits coming as surprises, leaving you more connected than ever before. Here's how it happened with Mary and Alicia. They were a couple in their late fifties, as different as night and day, but deeply connected.

Mary worked in a men's prison. She talked and moved with a gruff, direct confidence, and I could tell that no inmate could intimidate her. Yet when it came to Alicia, she would melt into softness and vulnerability. Alicia, who was a nurse, wove poetic mysteries as she talked, her face shifting with light and feeling.

They considered themselves survivors. Alicia's mother had jumped off a bridge after she put Alicia on the bus for her first day of kindergarten. Alicia lived with different family members while her mother was recovering. No one told her what happened. She wondered inside how bad she was for her mother to leave her. Mary was close to her father, handing him tools while he did his electrical work. Then he started drinking. He yelled insults at her and her mother at night, and spoke to them kindly the next morning. Mary learned to mistrust words. She decided she would be different from her father—she would always mean what she said and keep her word.

Mary and Alicia had moved in together eight years previously. Alicia put all her savings into financing a grand addition to Mary's house. Mary worked every weekend and after work, creating the 400-square-foot vaulted-ceiling kitchen and dining area that Alicia had always dreamed of. "We're a couple now," she thought to herself as she whistled and pounded nails. "I'm giving Alicia what she needs."

One day, Alicia's sister came over to help paint. Mary handed her a paint can. The sister refused to take it, pointing to another can, saying, "That's the color that Alicia wants." Mary, in her direct manner, replied, "This is our house, not yours, and I know what Alicia wants." The sister, surprised at Mary's directness, started to cry and ran to call Alicia.

When Alicia came home that night, she said to Mary, "I don't know if I can be in a relationship with someone who treats my family that way." Mary's world crashed in around her, and her joy in sharing partnership vanished. She said repeatedly to Alicia during couples therapy, "You don't choose me. You're more committed to your family than to me. I don't know if I can get over this. I have to be cold to protect myself." Alicia struggled to understand Mary's point of view and to prove her devotion, but nothing changed. They talked about many different issues in couples therapy, but they always went back to the paint can incident. They were beginning to think it couldn't be resolved and considered breaking up, even though they loved each other.

Then one day the creativity of Self energy emerged in their dialogue. They were trying to resolve financial issues, and I suggested they pay more attention to their parts than to the content of what they were saying. I encouraged them to slow down and to notice how it felt inside when they heard each other speak.

> Alicia: We have unfinished business about money. I'd like us to make plans and carry them through.
>
> Mary: I want it cleared up so we can talk when we need to.
>
> Alicia: You want to tell me what to do and you don't consult me. I'm scared I'll lose power.
>
> Mary: I'm stupid. I sold myself cheaply. I didn't acknowledge my own worth and value, and now I'm paying the price. When you bought into this property, my heart opened up to you and I thought it meant we would create a home. But you don't contribute your fair share of adult intimacy and commitment. I've been shortchanged. You go back to your mom and dad, and there's that famous remark you made, "I don't know if I can be in a relationship with someone who treats my family that way."

Following my directions, Alicia paused to notice how she felt inside. I thought she would be confused and helpless, imploring Mary to believe she was committed. Instead, she admitted her part of the problem for the first time.

> Alicia: I was premature in combining our households. I didn't know I was unready to be in a relationship. Part of me just jumped in, and I thought someone would tell me what to do. I coerced myself to take action so I wouldn't miss the opportunity. My family could tell I was unsure and afraid.

Alicia paused before she went on. Mary was sitting straight up in her chair, looking bright and alive. She had tears in her eyes. Finally, she spoke. "That's all I need. That's all I need to heal. You've never admitted your part in it before. That's all I need."

The feeling between them was warm and lovely. They stood up and embraced each other, looking connected and happy. When they came back the next week, they sat together as close partners and told me they had gotten what they came for, and they were done with couples therapy for now.

No one needed to tell Alicia to admit her role in the problem. When she paused and looked inside, and included all her parts, her creativity naturally emerged. It was elegant and precise, and it went directly to Mary's heart. Those few moments of Self energy had healed a barrier between them.

It may be hard to believe that a few moments could heal something so entrenched, or that there weren't other issues Mary and Alicia needed to deal with. But whatever might come up for them in the future, they knew from this experience that they could access the creativity of Self energy.

Self Offers Connection in Place of Isolation

When parts aren't connected with Self, they are isolated. They live in their own little rooms with the doors closed, unaware that there are other rooms, or a backyard, or anything else in the world.

When they connect with Self energy, their narrow, claustrophobic existence fades away, and they see opportunities appearing all around them.

Do you remember how Edward's little boy relaxed when he noticed him? The little boy had been banging his head in the corner for so long, scared of his father and ashamed that his mother was mocking him. When Edward went to that corner and hugged him, the boy's world opened up. For the first time, he could walk away from his mother's mocking words. A few seconds of connection freed him from decades of distress. You will see the magic of connection in every example in this book. It is the key to helping parts feel relieved, relaxed, and open to new possibilities.

You Can Solve Any Problem with Self Energy

When clients walk into my office, no matter how distressed they are, I know that they have the resources within them to solve their problems. When they connect with the Self qualities of creativity, courage, calm, compassion, confidence, curiosity, connection, and clarity, no issue is unsolvable.

Carol, a 40-year-old graduate student, sat in her chair with her boyfriend, Dan, across from her. She was calm on the outside, but inside, she was panicked about whether Dan was the right one for her and worried that she was replicating her mother's negative attitude. At first, she didn't understand why she should focus on her parts. She had no idea about the Self energy that would be released if she did this. Here is what she said after twelve weeks of therapy:

> I feel whole, no awareness of parts or goal statements. The analytical voice is very subdued. I just spent two weekends with Dan. I felt quiet in the space with him—it's not resignation but an awareness of the space we occupy together. I'm just able to enjoy it. I still have the old questions about our relationship, but they don't make me feel panicky. The panic was a firewall between what was actually going on and my picture of how it should be. I feel comfortable now, and I trust that we'll figure it out together.

> Nothing inside me is new; it's just regrouped in a way that's accessible. My parts are all spread out like a fan in front of me instead of stacked up on top of each other, getting in the way and confusing me. I used to try to be less negative, but now I just feel calm. Now when something is bothering me, I know it's a part and I need to welcome it like a respected guest; that it has its role and it will be listened to. I tell my parts they are important and vital, and that I will respect them. They like hearing that.

Carol began her statement saying she felt whole with no awareness of her parts. Paradoxically, she achieved that by first focusing on her parts. She learned that if something bothered her, it was a part, and it needed attention. Once her parts got the attention they needed, they receded into a sense of wholeness and fluidity, and she recovered a calm relationship with her world.

Carol said, "Now my parts are all spread out like a fan in front of me, instead of stacked up on top of each other, getting in the way and confusing me." Once you notice and understand your parts, they relax. They alternate among themselves as naturally as your breath alternates between coming in and going out.

When Carol said, "Nothing inside me is new," she was expressing a central truth: you have everything you need within you. You don't need to acquire anything or learn new skills to overcome your problems. Your inner wisdom is sufficient. You don't need to teach your parts what to do differently, only to release them from jobs they thought they had to do.

Now that you understand the limitless potential of Self energy, you can use it to meet your Exiles, offer them unburdening, and create a shift in the negative cycles between you and your partner. Exercise 6 will help you do that.

Exercise 6: Meeting Your Exile in the Spaciousness of Self Energy

1. Go back to the Exile you found in Exercise 4. Do you see or feel this part within you or beside you? Look at where it is living and

what is happening around it. Is it frightened of something? Is it feeling hurt, ignored, or misunderstood? Just notice the scene your Exile is showing you. If your heart is open to your Exile, let it know. Tell it you are there with it and that things can change. Write what happens below.

_____

_____

_____

2. If you cannot find your Exile and get to know it, it could be that another part is worried or doesn't trust you. Ask what the worry is or why it doesn't trust you to be with the Exile.

_____

_____

_____

_____

_____

3. See if you can calm the worry or distrust and get permission to approach your Exile. Try to meet your Exile and offer connection and compassion. Let it feel your confidence and courage. Invite it to communicate anything it wants to. Ask your Exile if it would like to lean into you and feel the qualities of Self energy. What happens?

_____

_____

_____

_____

_____

Your Exile may experience unburdening and feel free, light, and playful. If this doesn't happen, or if it happens only partially, you may benefit from the assistance of an IFS therapist. He or she can help you stay focused and gently deal with any obstacles. See "About Internal Family Systems" at the back of this book for contact information.

Now that you know about Self energy, you are ready to learn how to change reactive, unproductive cycles in your relationship while they are happening—by giving better back to your partner.

CHAPTER 6
Giving Better Back

Giving better back is a practical tool that will help you when you are most upset with your partner. When he or she is critical, judgmental, unfair, unreasonable, controlling, disconnected, disrespectful, or selfish, you can respond with more connection, calm, clarity, and compassion than you are getting.

You probably remember moments between you and your partner when everything seemed broken. Maybe your partner was angry, unfair, or unaware of your needs, and you couldn't find your way back to connection. Giving better back will help you make those broken moments whole and allow new experiences to replace repetitive old patterns.

When your partner is doing something you don't like, it's so easy to think, "He is so hurtful. I have to get angry back or go off in a huff to show him how bad he is." Instead, you can respond with better energy than you are getting. "Better" can mean many different things. Perhaps you will be more connected, more direct, more confident, or more compassionate than your partner. Better doesn't necessarily mean saying "nice things," or saying what you think your partner wants to hear, but rather saying or doing things that make you feel more whole or more present.

Whenever you are feeling poorly treated and you hear yourself thinking something like, "She doesn't deserve anything good from me because she isn't giving me anything good," I suggest you turn it upside down and think, "What could I give back that would be better than I'm getting?" When there is:

Criticism, you can be curious
Agitation, you can be calm
Judgment, you can be compassionate
Anxiety, you can be confident
Fear, you can be courageous
Confusion, you can be clear
Distance, you can be connected
Repetition, you can be creative

Giving better back is a good way to show your partner what you want by doing it. Your actions and attitude—connected, compassionate, clear—show your partner how it feels to be treated well. Your generosity is likely to be infectious. Your partner may think, "I like how it feels when she treats me this way. I want to treat her the same way."

Giving Better to Your Partner Is Also Giving Better to Yourself

Giving better back is as much for you as for your partner. When you send negative reactions to your partner, no matter how justified you feel and no matter who started it, you actually generate that same negativity within yourself. Blame, shame, and rejection don't just fly out toward your partner and leave you. They cause agitation or tension that remains with you. When you remove negativity from your response to your partner, you are also removing it from yourself. You will like yourself better and will feel more serene. Giving better to your partner is also giving better to yourself.

If Only You Would Do What I Want

You might think, "But I feel so much better when my partner does what I like. Why can't he or she just do it?" Often when people think this way, they spend their time explaining, persuading, arguing, and demanding that their partners do what they want. Elizabeth, who sat in my office with her husband, Peter, thought this way.

> Elizabeth: I feel so good when Peter listens to me. When we went to a couples workshop and he did the listening exercise, my whole body relaxed.

Elizabeth had an innocent, plaintive expression on her face. She was yearning for something that seemed so simple and basic to her. She went on:

> Elizabeth: I came home the other day, and I told Peter the washing machine broke and I was frustrated. He said, "Did you call the repairman?" I told him I just wanted him to listen to me for a moment without solving the problem. Then he thought I was criticizing him and telling him he could never do anything right. Why can't he just listen for a minute?

It made sense to me that Elizabeth wanted to be heard. She was the forgotten, self-sufficient child of a widowed mother of three who used alcohol to cope with the stress. Elizabeth recalled her mother telling her, "I thought you didn't need me."

Peter's face was dark as Elizabeth talked. He said, "Did you think I wasn't interested in your feelings?" The words were rational and curious, but Peter looked angry and disconnected. I wondered if he was getting lost in his private maze of childhood memories. He had told us that he remembered his father telling him in many different ways that he was not good enough. I wondered if he was translating Elizabeth's words to mean "I failed. I'm not good enough." With Peter lost in confusion, anger, and inferiority, Elizabeth wasn't going to get the listening she wanted. I could imagine her getting angry and hopeless very quickly. Neither of them wanted this. I remembered asking them in the beginning of the session what they wanted to walk away with, and they both had said, "Hope."

After we went through the "giving better back" process, Elizabeth said to Peter:

> A part of me wants to pursue you to the ends of the earth to make you listen to me. But what I really want to say to you is that I would prefer it if you would take a moment out of problem solving and just listen to my feelings. I know you want to fix problems, and I appreciate it, but what's better for me is if you stop for a moment and just listen to my frustration.

Elizabeth's second response was "better" than what she was getting because it was calmer, clearer, and more connected and compassionate than what Peter was offering at the moment. She felt much better responding this way than she would have with anger, and she had the calmness to wait while Peter ratcheted down his anger. She also got the understanding she wanted, and she definitely would not have gotten it if she had responded with agitation and accusation.

Peter got up and gave her a hug. As they left the session, they were giving each other spicy looks, and I thought they might rediscover passion as well as hope.

Why Do *I* Have to Give Something Better Back?

You may be wondering: "Why is it up to me to give better back? Shouldn't my partner be giving better back, too? Why didn't Peter give better back?" Of course, it's up to both of you. Over time, giving better back has to be mutual for a relationship to be viable. But in the moment of disturbance with your partner, it's only up to you. You have one hundred percent responsibility for the outcome (as does your partner). Don't think about whether your partner is giving better back—just do it yourself.

When you are in a difficult interaction with your partner and you think he or she is acting badly, it is likely that your partner's Firefighters are present. They are the ones that are blaming, punishing, distancing, lecturing, or forcing you. They are protecting your partner from the person they think is hurting him or her—you. You have become the enemy. Once your partner's Firefighters have branded you, anything you say or do is suspect. Your ability to influence your partner is diminished. You may say or do something perfectly reasonable, and still get a bad response.

Giving better back gets you off the enemy list. If you give up explaining, protesting, or asking your partner to change, and focus completely on giving better back than you're getting, your partner's Firefighters won't have anybody to fight with.

Sometimes you may think you are the only one giving better back. You're the one offering apologies, being curious, or staying calm, and you think your partner isn't reciprocating. Before you come to a firm conclusion that your partner isn't reciprocating, consider that he or she may also be giving better back, but in his or her own way. Perhaps you do it in words and your partner does it with actions. Perhaps you offer thorough, specific apologies, and your partner offers a few heartfelt words. If you pay attention to what your partner is doing, you may notice that he or she is generous, attentive, and kind, but in a style different from your own.

Better Can Mean Clear, Confident, and Assertive

Giving better back means responding with more connection, calm, clarity, compassion, courage, and creativity than you are getting. Sometimes that can mean compassionately focusing on your partner's feelings, and at other times it can mean focusing on your own feelings. As long as you aren't judgmental, forcing, or disconnected, and you don't need your partner to change right away, you can say anything that is true for you.

When I think of the assertive side of giving better back, I think of Grace. She and Bill were in their fifties. Grace's demeanor was gentle, but she was fed up with Bill's angry outbursts. She had been distancing more and more, to the point that she was imagining her elderly years without Bill. She spent a lot of time in the bedroom alone, reading, just to get away from Bill's irritability. Bill was an architect who specialized in ecological residences. I thought of Cary Grant as Bill leaned back in his chair, crossed his legs with a cool, debonair attitude, and spoke with interesting phrases and literary allusions. He didn't seem aware of Grace's distress.

Grace described how Bill had gotten angry with her on the previous Saturday night when she was looking for a parking space on the way to a concert. She started looking for a spot on the way to the hall, and he wanted her to go to the hall and then start looking. Bill was complaining that Grace never listened to him. I could feel the conversation going downhill. I was just about to intervene and ask Bill to notice the parts that were critical and argumentative when Grace said, "I just want you to hear the impact it had on me."

Her face was gentle, but her eyes were clear and direct. There was no challenge in her voice, just her own truth. I wasn't thinking about intervening anymore because Grace had done it more powerfully than I ever could have. She had given better back with clarity, courage, confidence, and connection. Bill stopped his minor rant and looked down. He had nothing to fight against because Grace wasn't forcing him to do anything. He couldn't ignore her because she was clear and connected.

Grace stood up to Bill without making him bad. She wasn't agitated, nor was she holding back. Her calm and truthfulness communicated her experience to Bill.

Better can mean being more confident and clear than your partner. If you feel hurt by something your partner did, you can ask yourself before you respond, "Am I feeling connected? Am I calm? Am I ready to stay calm no matter how my partner responds? Am I confident and clear about what I have to say?" If you answer yes, you can make an effective assertive statement.

Better Means Not Forcing Change

Trying to force your partner to change never works. No matter how sure you are that your partner is doing something bad, using force is not a "giving better back" response.

There are many ways to force your partner. Whether it's through criticizing, shaming, lecturing, punishing, bribing, threatening, or raging, if you override your partner's free will and try to impose your will on him or her, you're using force.

Your message is less effective when you use force to convey it. Your partner will focus more on resisting you and may not even understand what you are saying. He or she will dismiss your input, thinking, "She's just having a tantrum. I'll ignore her," or, "He's being pushy. I don't have to cave in to that." Giving better back than you're getting eliminates this excuse and makes it more likely that your partner will hear what you have to say and change because he or she wants to.

You lose power when you try to force your partner. Forcing conveys the message that you won't be okay unless someone changes. Does your happiness really depend on someone else's actions? Or can you be peaceful and happy within yourself even if you aren't getting what you want?

If you say what you want clearly and observe how your partner responds, you're giving better back. If you can remain confident, open, and connected whether your partner changes or not, you're giving better back. If you can be curious about your partner's lack of change, you're giving better back.

You will learn more about advocating for change in your relationship in Chapter 10, *Feedback: The Other Side of the Coin.*

But Who Started It?

In any committed relationship, a web of communication exists between partners, and it's often hard to tell who started a fight. Who is the hurt one and who did the hurting? You may think you were completely innocent and later find out that you said something that offended your partner.

It doesn't matter who started it. At any given moment, both partners can feel wronged—and both have the opportunity to give better back. Taking this opportunity is more productive than dwelling on who started it.

Giving better back prevents you from making a bad situation worse. Once something painful or unpleasant has happened, you cannot erase it. But you can avoid making it worse. This might seem like a small thing, but it is really a generous and radical act. Imagine what it would be like if you were irritated about your own life and took it out on your partner, and he stayed calm? Or if you forgot your anniversary and your partner was light-hearted about it? Something bad happened, but your partner didn't make it worse.

We Shouldn't Have Bad Times Anymore

Even if your partner changes his or her behavior at one point, the old ways might come back. Even when things are going well, something can always come up that hurts you. This may sound pessimistic, but if you accept this possibility, you will be better prepared for it. Giving better back will help you when you are surprised by a setback. Here's an example from Maria and John. They are a married couple in their forties who were in couples therapy with me. They came in one day and Maria told this story:

> John hasn't been critical for a while, and it has been heavenly. We've been as happy as we were on our honeymoon. But when we were cleaning up the basement the other day, he started to get nasty when I was taking too long deciding if I should throw things out. The old critical John was back. I felt hammered into the ground, and I started thinking about spending the evening alone with a book. I felt the old distancing feeling inside me.
>
> But I knew the way out was to give better back. So instead of going cold and distant, I described what was going on with me. I said, "I feel so drained. That really hurt. Everything you are saying sounds negative to me. I got used to you being nice to me, and now this feels like such a shock. I don't know why it is affecting me so much."
>
> I actually was interested in why I lost so much energy. My usual way would be to drift off somewhere, looking as though I

was fine but feeling judgmental inside. I like that I can give better back no matter what happens and maybe even learn something about myself.

I knew Maria was treading on dangerous ground when she called John critical. His face was hard to read, and I didn't know if he would admit he had been sharp with her or say something that felt critical to Maria. Maria was glowing with her achievement, and I felt relaxed, thinking that whatever John said, she could maintain her equanimity. She didn't need his approval for what she said because she felt the goodness of it within herself.

A few seconds after Maria finished, John spoke. "Yeah, I don't like it when you go away. I could tell when I was talking to you in the basement that you weren't there anymore. It was as though I was talking to myself. You always say I'm criticizing you when I'm just trying to give you some feedback. "

I had my answer to how John would respond. He focused more on his own disappointment and complaints than on Maria's feelings. I wondered to myself why he couldn't examine his own behavior.

I didn't intervene and question John because I was hoping that Maria would be able to handle it herself. I sat back as she looked at him, calm, attentive, and connected. Her face looked soft, and I saw compassion in her eyes. This wasn't a mutual conversation—she admitted her faults and he didn't—but she was patient. She really wowed me with her next response to John: "I can see how it can be unsatisfying to share with me sometimes. I do go away when I feel threatened. Sometimes I do that with my friends, too, and I can see their eyes glaze over. Maybe I go away more than I realize."

John's eyes moistened. "Well, my dad had a lot of trouble being there for me. He was a social worker who gave more to his clients than to his own family. It left me feeling as though I just didn't know him. There was some part of him that was so distant. Once I rowed him out into the bay just so he couldn't get away. I wanted to ask him who he was."

Maria was there with John, silently connecting with him. The light was shifting on the rose-colored wall behind them and time seemed to stop. We were in a moment of pure being. I imagined I could see the energy of John's heart, soft with sadness about his father, tenderly held by Maria's presence. Maria had started it all with giving better back, even though she was disoriented by the return of old behaviors. She got far more in return than she would have gotten by distancing.

You Have to Connect to Give Better Back

Giving better back only works when you feel connected to your partner. If you respond with clarity and confidence, but you aren't connected, you won't reach your partner's heart. If you feel connected, you can say almost anything and get a good response. Perhaps you have parts that don't want you to connect with your partner. They might think you are safer if you stay distant because it won't hurt as much if your partner gets angry or ignores you. They might think that you couldn't tolerate a bad response from your partner.

Paradoxically, it will hurt less if you stay connected when your partner makes a hurtful response. When you are connected, pain can seem to flow *through* you rather than getting stuck *in* you. You have more access to your deeper resources when you are connected. You may surprise yourself with the compassion, creativity, and humor that arise when you stay connected.

How Far Do You Go in Giving Better Back?

As long as you want to stay in your relationship, keep giving better back. Observe how your partner responds. If you are giving better back and he or she doesn't change, that is data. You may want to stay, or you may want to move on.

If you want to end your relationship, keep giving better back until the moment you leave, and then move on with as little regret about your own behavior as possible.

Giving Better Back Is Your Natural State

Even though I am describing giving better back as something you can practice, it is not a skill you have to learn. It's your natural state. You always have the ability to treat others well, no matter how they are treating you. Even if you are standing up for yourself, you can do it with respect for the other person. Here is good news: when you pay attention to your Exiles, your natural goodness emerges. Your protectors will relax and let you fearlessly interact with all that is in front of you.

Soon you will have the opportunity to practice giving better back. Let's start with the list of qualities in the beginning of the chapter. They are the Self qualities that Schwartz (1995, 2001, 2004) describes in the Internal Family Systems model.

Curious
Calm
Compassionate
Confident
Courageous
Clear
Connected
Creative

Before you respond to your partner, you'll be checking yourself for Self qualities. Are you curious? Are you calm? Are you compassionate? Are you confident, courageous, clear, connected, and creative? If you answer no to any one of these questions, you can adjust your tone or your words.

You will also be asking yourself, "What is my partner doing or not doing that is hurting me right now? Is she ignoring me, judging me, pushing me, humiliating me, misunderstanding me, or trying to control me?" Whatever it is, you can do the opposite back. Instead of ignoring, you can reach out. Instead of criticizing, you can ask for a clarification. Instead of humiliating, you can be respectful. Instead of trying to make your partner stop pushing you, you can calmly express your preference.

You can use the immediate hurt you are feeling to guide your "better" response. If you are getting something you don't like, you can give back less of it. If you are missing something, you can give what you wish you were getting.

You don't have to change yourself or learn to speak carefully—the information you need is already within you. You know what is disturbing you. You can use that as your pivot point, and move from disconnection to connection, from forcing to respect, and from judgment to compassion.

In Exercises 7 and 8 at the end of this chapter, you can practice giving better back. Here's how Raphael and Courtney did the exercise.

Raphael and Courtney Practice Giving Better Back

Raphael and Courtney were back in couples therapy after a year's hiatus, with Courtney six months pregnant. In our third session, Raphael sat slumped and despondent in his chair with a mild, sweet expression on his face. I remembered him telling me that he had learned, as an African immigrant in Oakland, to keep a pleasant demeanor so white people wouldn't be anxious or think he was stealing something.

Courtney was shifting with emotion. Her eyes, skin, and even her bones seemed to express what she felt. I had just asked her how satisfied she was with the marriage, on a scale of one to ten. She had answered, "Five. I need to see profound change in how Raphael sees me." The low number shocked me. What had I missed in the couples therapy a year ago? Why wasn't her expressiveness helping her communicate what she needed to Raphael? I decided that I would focus on giving better back and invite them to practice it at home in a consistent, disciplined way.

I gave them both sheets of paper with the following questions.

What my partner does that bothers me

What I don't like about it

What I'd rather my partner would do
I looked at Raphael's sheet. It said:

What my partner does that bothers me:
She doesn't acknowledge me for what I do well.
She tells me not to play Game Boy at night.

What I don't like about it:
It's demeaning.

What I'd rather my partner would do:
I'd rather have an affirmation.

We started with Raphael. I explained that giving better back for him would mean giving back something better than demeaning and more like the affirmation he wished he were getting. I asked Courtney to repeat her critical comments about Game Boy so Raphael could practice giving better back. After she did, he replied, "I affirm you for holding the highest expectations for our relationship."

Raphael's words were elegant and stately, and I wondered if he felt Self qualities when he said them. I asked Raphael how he felt, and he answered, "I feel higher and I don't feel 'poor me.'" He checked for the presence of Self qualities and they were all there. He was sitting straight in his chair, looking vibrant, present, and happy with himself. This was the right response for Raphael.

Now it was Courtney's turn. She had written:

What my partner does that bothers me:
I ask him for a favor and he says yes, if I do what he wants. He's selfish and immature. He's disconnected and isolated.

What I don't like about it:
He doesn't follow the rules of conduct.

What I'd rather my partner would do:
I wish he would act like an adult. I want to feel heard. I want to feel connected.

Her "giving better back" goal was to be unselfish, mature, and connected, and to follow the rules of conduct. For practice, Raphael made a statement about doing a favor only if she did something he wanted. She responded, "I choose you every day, morning, noon, and night." When I asked her to check for Self qualities, she said, "I don't feel any of them."

"Okay," I said, "Try again. What do you feel when he says he'll do you a favor only if you do something for him?" She answered:

Courtney: Bewildered.

Mona: Okay, instead of bewildered, what would you like to feel?

Courtney: Connected. Like I've been heard.

Mona: Okay, give that back.

Courtney (silent for a moment): I'd rather you do the favor without asking for anything back.

Mona: How was that?

Courtney: Clear, connected, and acknowledging.

Mona: Do you feel the Self qualities?

Courtney (calm and self-assured): They are all there. I get it. Giving better back doesn't mean being grand and it doesn't mean idealizing. It doesn't have to be wishful thinking.

Courtney learned that giving better back doesn't mean saying what you think you should say. It means saying what helps you feel fully present, connected, compassionate, and calm. Being grand or idealizing didn't work for her, but being assertive did. Looking for Self qualities guided her to the right response.

Courtney and Raphael seemed hopeful as they gathered up their papers and agreed to keep giving better back at home.

When they walked in the next week, I was alert for signs of progress or failure. Raphael's face looked different—I puzzled over the change and then noticed I could see his features more clearly, as if I were wearing stronger glasses. I realized that he had been hiding himself before. I remembered the stories he told about the dignity, pride, and jubilance his father had carried with him from Africa. "My father always wore a hat with a big feather, in Oakland, no less," he had said, "and he could pull it off." I thought to myself, "Raphael looks like a grown man and a father."

Raphael started. "We practiced giving better back. The first time was when I walked in and started going through the mail. Courtney said, 'I'd rather you talk to me before you go through the mail.' I just thought, 'Okay.' It was no big deal."

Courtney's simple, nonjudgmental request had allowed Raphael to change what he was doing without feeling bad or blamed, and he liked it.

Courtney continued. "The second time was when you were watching the Jim Jones documentary. I asked you if you were going to come to bed and you said, 'Yes,' but you stayed glued to the TV. I felt so lonely. I went to bed and cried. You came to bed, and I got up, went into the living room, and cried alone. You came to me and said, 'Would you like to cry alone or come to bed with your husband?' It was something about the way you said, 'husband.' I felt settled, like I have a husband, my baby's father is here. I wasn't scared anymore."

Courtney went on, "I realize that I keep score. I'm always comparing what you give with what I give and assigning bad marks. Now I know that if I keep score, we're going to fail."

It was clear to me how Courtney's expressiveness had failed to make an impact on Raphael—she always colored it with judgment and scorekeeping. When she made the subtle, powerful adjustment of giving better back, she got her needs across and brought both herself and Raphael into loving relationship.

Exercises 7 and 8 will help you develop your own "giving better back" response. The exercises are done alone at first, without input from your partner. When you get to Question 5 in Exercise 8, you will have the opportunity to try out your response with your partner.

Exercise 7: Giving Better Back, Part I

The first part of giving better back is to find the Firefighter that
wants to respond to the hurt.

1. What does your partner do that bothers you (such as a word, a
    behavior, or something else)?

    _____

    _____

    _____

    _____

    _____

    _____

2. Find the Firefighter that wants to respond to this bothersome
    behavior. This would be the angry, demeaning, distancing,
    punishing, forcing, or hopeless response that you might be
    thinking of. Describe what your Firefighter wants to do and
    how it wants to do it.

    _____

    _____

    _____

    _____

    _____

3. Connect with and acknowledge your Firefighter. Offer it un-
    derstanding for what it is trying to do. Ask it if it will trust you
    to handle the situation in another way. If it refuses, ask it why.
    You may be led to an Exile and have to unburden it before you
    get permission to do things differently. You can refer back to
    Exercises 3 and 4 if you need to do this.

    _____

    _____

    _____

    _____

Exercise 8: Giving Better Back, Part 2

After you have found your Firefighter(s), and obtained their go-ahead, you can figure out your "giving better back" response.

1. What is it about your partner's behavior that bothers you? For each negative thing, write what you would rather get from your partner. For example: insulting-respectful, uncommitted-committed, manipulative-direct, selfish-cooperative, deceitful-honest, or critical-appreciative.

    _____
    _____
    _____
    _____
    _____
    _____

2. Use this information to figure out how to give better back. How could you give the quality you wish you were receiving? What could you say? What tone could you use?

    _____
    _____
    _____
    _____
    _____
    _____

3. Imagine giving the response you wrote in Question 2. Check to see if you have all the qualities below. Remember, if you are trying to force your partner to do something, you won't be able to access Self qualities.

    ___ Curiosity   ___ Courage
    ___ Calm   ___ Clarity
    ___ Compassion   ___ Connection
    ___ Confidence   ___ Creativity

4. Are any Self qualities missing? If so, adjust your "giving better back" response. Keep scanning yourself for Self qualities
   until they are all there. Write your final "giving better back"
   response below.

   _____

   _____

   _____

   _____

   _____

5. Now you are ready to offer your "giving better back" response
   to your partner. Notice how you feel while you give it. Notice
   how your partner responds. Write your observations below.

   _____

   _____

   _____

   _____

   _____

Giving Better Back and Taking Care of Your Exiles: A Way of Life

Sometimes you might try to give better back and revert to
impatience, judgment, distance, anger, disconnection, or addictions
(your Firefighter behaviors). This is an opportunity to go back to
Exercise 6 and get to know your Exiles. Remember, whenever
Firefighters come out, it means there is a hurt Exile. If you can
find it, notice it, and acknowledge its pain, your Firefighters won't
have to attack or distance.

If you keep taking care of your Exiles and practicing giving
better back, you will get used to a free, happy state of mind, and
to loving, compassionate connection with your partner. You will
be better able to notice when these qualities are missing. You
may feel your heart closing up, hear yourself thinking judgmental
thoughts, or lose a vibrant sense of connection with your partner.

These are signals that an Exile has been triggered and a protector is waking up. You know you can find your Exile and help it feel less alone and frightened. The more you notice these nuances in yourself, the more you can do to stop negative spirals in your relationship and offer love that fulfills both you and your partner.

Getting to know your Exiles and giving better back can become a way of life. You will always have a way out of lonely, isolated, and unhappy relationship cycles, and access to tools to restore calm and confidence within yourself.

Now let's learn how to keep choice alive and vibrant in your relationship over the years.

CHAPTER 7

Keep Choice Alive

When you keep choice active and alive, you will be able to say to your partner after ten, twenty, or fifty years, "Knowing all that I know now, having been through good times and bad, and being with you in your worst moments and best moments, I still choose you over all others." Would you like to live with this kind of active, evolving, vibrant choice?

When relationships begin, choice is easier. Your new partner seems different and better than the other people you have met. You are hopeful that he or she will care how you feel, accept you as you are, keep you safe and secure, and give you all the excitement you need. In the beginning of a relationship, you don't have to think about maintaining choice.

The passage of years together can tarnish this experience. Partners can feel hurt or disappointed with each other, the same bad things can keep happening, and bad times can overshadow good times. Partners try to change each other, but the hurt continues. Choice is no longer clear and bright. Partners might think, "Now that I know who you are, maybe I wouldn't have chosen you. But I'm here, so I guess I'll stay."

Here is the secret to enjoying active, vital relationship choice over time: the intense distress you feel when your partner does hurtful things is really your own Exile pain. As you learned in Chapter 4, "If it's intense, it's your own." When you encounter one of these painful experiences, say to yourself, "This is about me. If it's intense, it's my own."

If you are disturbed or hurt and you can stay calm, connected, confident, and creative when you express yourself, it's different. Your Firefighters haven't been triggered, and there is no hurting Exile behind them. Then it's time for feedback—you'll learn more about that in Chapter 10.

If you can find your hurt parts, stay with them, acknowledge them, and help them get free of the past, you won't have to feel as much pain when your partner hurts you. You will feel hurt, but not the sudden overwhelming hurt of Exiles. You'll feel only moderate pain, and as you'll find out in Chapter 10 on feedback, you'll be able to convey your reactions productively. When you are free of all-consuming Exile pain, you can fortify your choice, renew your commitment, and enjoy your partner for who he or she is. You can have a radiant "attitude of gratitude."

Example: Leticia's Panic Comes from an Old Wound

Let's see how Leticia, a secretary in a construction firm, met a challenge in her three-year-old marriage. During one couples therapy session, she sat across from her husband, Terrence, unable to get coherent words out, almost unable to breathe. She had just asked him how much money they were saving. Terrence answered factually, but his emotions were flat, and he seemed a bit annoyed.

> Terrence: It depends on what the judge says about the alimony my ex wants.
>
> Leticia (with gulps of air): It's always like this. He can't get away from his old family. It's as though we aren't a real couple. He doesn't set limits with his ex-wife, so I never know where we are.

Since we had already had several sessions, Leticia understood that the breathless panic she was feeling was her own and that it came from an Exile. Helping her focus and unblend, I asked, "Would it be okay to notice the panicky feeling inside your body?" Leticia went inside, her eyes softly focused on a spot five feet ahead of her on the rug. Noticing the feeling brought up a memory.

> I see myself at age ten. I'm sitting with my father on a green flowered couch. He just got married and moved in with his new wife and her kids. I'm visiting him after his honeymoon, and I'm so glad to see him again. I'm cuddling up to him and he has his arm around me. He's saying, "Wow, you got picked for the choir. That's great! You always had a beautiful voice, girl." I was acting embarrassed, but I really liked it. Then his new wife called from the other room to remind him to look for a cooler they needed for their trip to the beach the next day. At first I felt good, thinking that I liked going to the beach with my dad, and how we played ball on the sand. Then I realized that I was going back to my mom's house in the morning. I felt horrible, thinking my dad was going to the beach without me. I had felt special at the wedding because they included me and all my relatives were there paying attention to me, and I sang a song. But all of a sudden, I didn't feel special anymore. It was as though I was floating and there wasn't any ground under me. I didn't say anything because I didn't want to ruin it for my father. I thought I had to be strong and tough and deal with it on my own.

When Terrence mentioned his ongoing alimony dispute in response to her question about savings, Leticia felt the old loss of feeling special to her father. To her, Terrence's reference to the judge meant he was abandoning her and putting his old family before her. Leticia's voice was softer as she went on.

> That's when I started having anxiety. I didn't want to go out much or make new friends. Actually, that's when I started counting things to calm myself down. That's a big secret. No one knew.

Terrence's alimony dispute was a big challenge for Leticia. It brought back old feelings of abandonment, anxiety, and loss of identity. She had to meet this challenge to keep her relationship with Terrence alive. After she came out of her sad memories, she went back to the dialogue with Terrence. Her face was full of feeling, but she was calm and firm at the same time. She said to him, "I want you to know that I am your family now. We have our own finances, and I'd like to know more about our savings." Now Terrence was listening to her. They started talking about how he was handling the alimony and court dispute, and ways that he was colluding to let his ex-wife keep controlling him. He looked relieved to be getting it all out.

If Leticia hadn't found the Exile that was hurt from loss of special attention, she would have continued to panic and blame Terrence for the way he was handling his ex-wife. She probably would have had thoughts about whether she had chosen the right husband. If the conflict about finances and alimony kept recurring, she and Terrence might have become a distant, discouraged couple over time. Instead, they were back to active, alive choice.

Choice: Mining the Depths of Your Capacity for Love

When you commit to keeping your choice alive, your capacity for love will be tested. The challenges that arise will call you to find deeper resources.

What if your partner isn't as warm, generous, exciting, or appreciative as you wish he or she was? Maybe you are saying to yourself, "I would be more loving if he was warmer ," "I would be open if she understood me better," or "I would share more of my exciting side if he was more receptive." You might even imagine that you could give your best with someone else.

But when you commit to one person, that's who you have to love. You are challenged to bring your love to a particular person with particular characteristics. You are challenged to find a way to offer the best love you have to your partner as he or she is.

The Relationship Web

When you choose one person, you create a unique web of inter-actions formed by the combination of your characteristics and your partner's characteristics. A web with any one person will have particular joys and challenges, different from the web with anyone else. That's because you bring your parts to all your relationships, but different people meet them differently. The web with your partner cannot be duplicated with anyone else. Perhaps someone else could give you some of the same experiences, but not all of them.

Choosing your partner means choosing him or her as is, with all the things you like and all the things that frustrate you. You can't mix and match, insert, or delete qualities to make a custom-blended partner. Choosing a partner means choosing the whole package. The following exercise will help you visualize active choice with your partner as he or she is.

Exercise 9: The Web

Picture you and your partner on opposite sides of a web or a net, a meadow, or a starfield in the sky. Take your time and find the right image for your relationship.

Now see your parts moving in across the field, net, or starfield from your side, and your partner's parts doing the same from his or her side. Maybe you see little versions of yourself moving across, or you see colors, sounds, words, or shapes.

Look at where your parts and your partner's parts meet. What do those meeting points look like? Are they knots in a net? Nodes in a web? Do they have colors or shapes, or do you see you and your partner there?

Look at the negative ones first—the ones where your parts and your partner's parts combine in a difficult or frustrating way. What do they look or sound like?

Focus on what your parts are doing. Are they saying something? Do they have a tone or a posture? What do they believe? What one word best sums up their experience?

Now shift and look at the positive meeting places. Notice which of your own parts are happy in those places. What are they doing? What are they saying? How do they look? Is there a word that expresses the happiness in those places? Take a breath and see what your body feels like.

Now go back to the negative meeting places. Imagine Self qualities (curiosity, calm, connection, confidence, creativity, compassion, courage, and clarity) coming from your side and flowing to the disturbing places. Your partner's contribution remains the same. The only change is in you. What is the meeting place like now? How do your parts react to your Self energy? What is different? How does your body feel?

What do the connections in the web look like? Are they like the knots in a net? Do they have colors or shapes, or do you see yourself and your partner meeting there? First notice the positive meeting places. What do they look like? Watch, listen, and feel how they manifest the positive joining of you and your partner. Are there words, images, sounds, or feelings there? Notice if one particular place is the most radiant. Notice how your body feels when you focus on the positive meeting places.

Now notice the inflamed meeting places where you and your partner combine in a difficult or frustrating way. What do your parts look, sound, or feel like? Are they saying something?

Focus on your own part in the inflamed connection. What does it look like? How is it responding to your partner? What does it believe? Is there a particular word that comes to you?

Write your experiences below:
Positive connections:

_____

_____

_____

_____

Negative connections:

_____

_____

_____

_____

How my parts changed with Self qualities:

_____

_____

_____

The negative intersections in your net are your roadmap for growth. With someone else, you might have different intersections because the combination of qualities would be different. When you choose one partner, you are choosing a particular set of opportunities and challenges.

When you understand that any relationship web will have challenges, you don't have to think about leaving when you face conflict or frustration. You can meet the challenge, knowing that you'd have the same level of difficulty, if not the same type of difficulty, with anyone else.

If you don't keep choice alive in your relationship, you might divert your attention to children or work, accept a dull commitment to longevity, enjoy the temporary solace of addictions, distract yourself with affairs, or resign yourself to a life without a vital couple connection. It doesn't have to be that way.

Who You Choose Is How You Grow

As you may have seen from your relationship web, your partner challenges you in specific ways. You can protest, saying to yourself that you didn't sign on for this or that you'd be happier with someone else. Or you can choose the challenge. Would you like to see who you would become if you accepted your relationship challenges as your own? Would you like to see what new capacities you would develop?

The person you choose as your partner influences who you will become and which of your qualities will grow and fortify. The challenges he or she provides focus your growth in specific directions. Will you become more assertive or more receptive? Will you learn to be alone without feeling abandoned, or will you learn to connect without losing yourself? Will you learn to accept love, or will you learn to reach out more? Will you learn to maintain your confidence when you are criticized, or will you learn to bear frustration without criticizing? In short, who you choose is how you grow.

Actively choosing your partner over time means choosing to meet the particular challenges he or she brings you, and being able to say to yourself, "I didn't know these challenges would be here when I began this relationship, but here they are. This is interesting. If I stay with you, I'll learn to be more generous, assertive, clear,compassionate, adventurous, etc. These are things I need to learn anyway."

When you live by the principle "If it's intense, it's my own," you can keep choice alive in your relationship. You can say to yourself on a daily basis, "I would choose you again. This relationship brings me richness I could not get with any other person. I like the person I have become through meeting the challenges you bring me."

Still Looking for a Partner?

You can use your understanding of relationship choices and challenges to find a new partner. Since you know that all committed, intimate relationships bring a mixture of challenges and satisfactions, you expect that any potential partner is going to trigger you and throw you into a tailspin at some point. You can ask yourself, "What part of me is getting triggered? What's in the way of me staying connected and clear no matter what he or she does?"

Find the part of you that gets triggered and get to know it. Do you feel excited and proud of yourself? Was the process interesting to you? Notice how your prospective partner is responding to you. Is he or she aware of your shift? Can you feel a change in the energy between the two of you? Even if your partner doesn't say the exact right words, does it feel better?

If you try to evaluate the relationship before you have found your own triggered part, you will miss the opportunity to find out how your partner would respond if you were able to stay calm, clear, and connected.

If you keep having the same unhappy experience with different partners, consider that you have a part that is used to a certain kind of relationship. You can get to know this part and find out how it got used to this pattern. When you do, you'll be able to free yourself from repetitive attraction to relationships that keep going down the same dreary road.

Do you feel torn between different types of partners? Does one part of you want someone stable and another part want someone creative and expressive? Does one part want a devoted partner and another one seek someone indifferent or apathetic to you? Parts often come in pairs of opposites. If you have a set of contradictory parts, look inside and get to know them. Listen to their opposing points of view, one at a time, and find out why they have to be so polarized. When you use the tools you learned in Exercises 3, 4, and 5, you'll hear the stories that make your parts alternate between opposites and you'll be able to help them relax and trust you to try new ways.

Do you find a lot of possible partners but stop short of choosing one? Are you worried about losing your independence or your attraction to other people? If you find yourself on a merry-go-round of wanting to commit and not being able to, you probably have parts that are stuck with old pain. As you learned in Exercise 6, you can go inside and find out if any parts think commitment is dangerous. Maybe you will find an Exile that learned that you should never trust people because they will always go away, or that you will be hurt no matter what you do.

When you free your stuck Exiles from their limited beliefs, you will expand your options. Perhaps that will mean you will commit to one partner. Or perhaps you will decide to accept the richness of your single life. Regardless, you can make the choice from a place of freedom rather than from the small, confined rooms in which your Exiles live.

You have learned the importance of keeping choice alive in your relationship through meeting your specific relationship challenges. In the next chapter, you will learn how Managers, Exiles, and Firefighters influence your partner choice, what happens when one part dominates the choice, and how it affects the challenges you face.

CHAPTER 8
Different Parts Choose
Different Partners

I deally, Managers, Exiles, and Firefighters enrich your partnership choice. Managers will remind you about the need for security and safety, Exiles will tell you when they think someone
can meet emotional needs that have gone unmet for too long, and
Firefighters advocate for excitement and intensity.

Sometimes all three parts work together, and you choose a
partner who brings a gratifying blend of safety, emotional depth,
and excitement. But when Managers, Exiles, or Firefighters have
fallen into extreme roles, they add extreme input to the choice
process. Sometimes just one part makes the choice, skewing
the relationship toward safety, the dream of deep emotional
reparation, or excitement.

Let's start with Managers and see what happens when safety is
the primary concern in a relationship.

Managers Choose Safety

When you are evaluating a partner, your Managers ask, "Is this
relationship safe and comfortable? Will we have a predictable
life? Will we have financial security? Will we avoid the things that
hurt us in the past?"

Managers are primarily concerned with avoiding pain. They
care more about avoiding something bad than getting something

good. Because of their absorption with avoidance, they may choose someone who doesn't do the bad things but who lacks other important qualities. For instance, if you missed emotional attention when you were young, Managers might be attracted to someone who consistently nurtures and attends to you and fail to notice that he can't hold a job. If one or both of your parents were violent, Managers might focus on a kind, generous person, and ignore that she can't vary enough from her usual routines to take a vacation or go to a concert. If you were devastated by losing someone important to you at a young age, Managers might choose someone faithful and dependable who would never leave you and discount the lack of interesting conversation.

For example, Arthur's father taught him to avoid doing things that would displease people. He often said, "Don't make waves; think about how you look to others." Arthur remembered being seven years old and coming home happy after a baseball game. He told his father how he had slid into home plate and scored a run, waving his slightly bruised elbow as he spoke. "Why were you playing?" his father asked. "Now you'll look bad when the neighbors come over for the barbecue." Arthur's happy feelings evaporated. He knew his father was telling him, "Don't have fun if it causes people to notice you." He never heard, "Have a good time" or "Think about what's important to you." It was only, "What looks good to others?"

Arthur chose a mate the only way he could—according to other people's expectations. His family liked her, her hobbies were socially acceptable, and she supported his career. He never thought to himself, "Do I feel excited with her? Do I feel deeply connected? Does she give me the love I've always wanted?"

Thirty years of marriage later, Arthur found himself walking around the house moody and distracted. He couldn't feel any joy or connection with his wife, Rachel, and it no longer mattered to him that she created a nice home, that they had nice friends, and that they were respected in the community. He said, as he and Rachel sat in my office, "For the first time in my life, I want to pay attention to what I need. You're not spontaneous and you don't initiate things." She leaned toward him, tears in her eyes, trying to understand what he meant. The next week she showed up at his office in a trench coat—and nothing else. But no matter what she did or said, he felt dead inside, and she felt helpless, inadequate, and confused.

Arthur had chosen his wife with only one part: a Manager. Repeating what he had heard from his father, his Manager said to him, "Above all, please others." Years later, when he discovered he wanted to please himself, too, his marriage felt empty and dreary to him, and he couldn't appreciate the efforts his wife was making to change.

I noticed that when Arthur told Rachel that he wanted her to be more spontaneous, his emotions were flat. I had to remind myself that this topic had supreme importance in his life. Why wasn't he communicating the urgency of his need for a more stimulating, self-starting partner? It wasn't until we went back in time to Arthur's childhood that we learned how well he had learned to hide his needs. Arthur had to find the Exile that was hurt from pervasive fearfulness that came through the generations, from his great-grandfather to his grandfather to his father and now to him. Once he did, he could allow more emotion into his words. Then Rachel got the impact and in turn began to question herself. She realized that he wasn't asking for something that looked like spontaneity, but rather something that actually came out of her own *joie de vivre*. She began to talk about how her own family had taught her to hide her vitality. She took her own journey into the past, away from fear and into courage and aliveness.

Exiles Yearn for What They Never Had

Exiles are the parts that feel the pain from past experiences. They live in the rooms, porches, or hallways where it happened, never growing up, cycling through the same scenes. Their existence is miserable, and they would love a way out. Exiles want your partner to provide it.

Exiles think a partner is a second chance to get the good feelings they always dreamed of. If you were wounded by neglect, your Exiles want attention. If you got inappropriate attention, they want respect and autonomy. If you heard that you couldn't do anything right, they want abundant praise and approval. When they get what they want from their partners, they feel deeply bonded. If your Exiles are happy, you might hear yourself saying, "I have found my soul mate and I am complete now." As long as your partner loves you the right way, all is very well.

The problem is that Exiles can't bear it when they don't get what they want. When they experience a moment of selfishness, criticism, or intrusiveness from your partner, they tumble from heaven into a bottomless pit. The disappointment is as huge as the satisfaction was. Exiles can't just say, "Ouch, honey, that hurt," with a smile and a light, humorous touch. To them, it's the end of the world. Exile love is precarious and stormy.

Exiles Seek the Familiar Even If It Is Bad

Exiles know they want good love, the opposite of the bad love they had in the past. But they, like all of us, can only do what they know. They know from the past that love means feeling abandoned, demeaned, or frightened. If they find someone who is present, supportive, and safe, they scratch their heads and think, "She's nice, but I don't feel attracted."

Whatever was there in early relationships, whether it was good or bad, becomes part of the shape of love. It's as if a template is created, holding the pattern for what love is. If there was abandonment, abandonment becomes part of the template. If there was criticism, that becomes part of the template. If there was rage and chaos, that is included in the template. When Exiles compare prospective partners to the template, they don't get a match unless the part-ners give them some abandonment, criticism, or rage.

Even though Exiles know how bad it is to feel abandoned, attacked, or demeaned, they are drawn to it. Otherwise, it doesn't click. It slides off them as if they were coated with Teflon. Exiles are in a terrible bind, desperately wanting good love but incapable of choosing it.

Old relationship templates program Exiles so effectively that they even see the old bad treatment when it isn't there. When they see their partner reading the paper at the breakfast table, coming to bed late, or staring off into the distance, they interpret it as abandonment because that's what they're used to. Maybe after a while partners will think to themselves, "Since you think I'm abandoning you no matter what I do, maybe I won't try anymore." Here is the tragedy of Exiles: they need good love, but they keep choosing, perceiving, and even creating the same hurtful experiences.

Remember, there is hope: you can find your Exiles, acknowledge them, and help them let go of their pain. Your partner cannot deliver your Exiles from their personal anguish—only you can do that. You can remind yourself, "If it's intense, it's my own." When you put this belief into action, you won't have to crash when your partner disappoints you. You will have a moment to think to yourself, "That hurt so much. It's intense, so it must be my own. Which of my Exiles is hurting?" You can pay attention and trace your reaction to its real cause—your Exile, not your partner.

Firefighters Choose Excitement

If Firefighters dominate relationship choice, the relationship will be full of energy and excitement. You will think to yourself, "She really keeps me interested. I won't ever lose my attraction. We do so many exciting things." You'll keep passion alive because you'll be willing to see your partner as slightly mysterious and suspend your need for security and predictability (Perel, 2006). You'll have the oxygen needed to soar into sensual altitudes.

When Firefighters lock into protective roles, they, like Managers, want to avoid pain. Their method is to flood you with intensity so that you can't feel emotional pain. They distract with intensity and block everything else out. When you are fighting, getting drunk, having affairs, or buying everything in the store, you usually aren't feeling unworthy or depressed. The activity commands your attention, so there is none left over for pain. When Firefighters rule partner choice, you get excitement but not security or emotional depth.

If you have made your partner choice with Firefighters leading, you will be faced with the challenge of going beyond intensity to find vulnerability. You will need to find the courage to stay with that vulnerability instead of distracting yourself from it. When you do, you'll be able to enjoy intensity but also have security and emotional depth.

If you know what parts were involved in your original relationship choice, you will understand the challenges you have to meet. You will know if you have to address your need for safety, your disappointment when deep needs are not met, or your need for intensity. You will know that extreme needs come from parts that think they need to rule your life. If you can find those parts and meet them in the places that formed their beliefs, you will have the option to include more variety and balance in your partnership.

CHAPTER 9
Caution: Firefighters at Work

As you may remember, Firefighters are the energetic protectors that jump out to distract you from Exile pain. When you and your partner are angry, critical, or distant, your Firefighters are running the show. The more you understand Firefighters, the more ability you will have to unravel your most negative couple cycles.

Curiosity is the best way to learn about your Firefighters. When you pay attention to them, you will find out what they are thinking and what they are trying to do. But sometimes it's hard to be curious about your Firefighters. You don't notice they are there—you're just immersed in anger or distance, and you have no room to think about what you're doing.

The Firefighter categories and descriptions in this chapter will help you recognize the wide range of Firefighter behaviors. You might realize that your Firefighters are working more frequently than you thought.

As you read this chapter, try to focus on your own Firefighters. You may be tempted to focus more on your partner's Firefighters, thinking to yourself, "That's what he does! That's what she's doing when she drives me crazy!" Noticing your partner's Firefighters won't help you. If you try to tell your partner about his or her Firefighters, you will probably find yourself in a fight or a stand-off.

Focus on your own Firefighters. Not only will it help you create and sustain intimacy in your relationship, it also will help you find peace within yourself.

Committed Relationships Wake Up Exiles

Marriages (and non-married partnerships) trigger Firefighters more than friendships or work relationships. Have you ever noticed that your partner can make you feel more helpless, angry, irrational, hopeless, or frustrated than anyone else? That's because adult partnerships are uniquely constellated to bring out your Exiles, and Firefighters follow right behind. That's because the exclusivity, closeness, and dependency of childhood are repeated in your adult partnership.

Your Parents and Your Partner: Exclusive, Close, and Dependent

Before adulthood, your parents were the people with whom you felt most exclusive, close, and dependent. You couldn't trade in your parents (or parent substitutes) for that nice Mrs. Jones down the block or that cool gym teacher. There was natural physical intimacy in feeding, dressing, and bedtime. When you needed clothes, food, or help with homework, it usually had to come from your parents.

When you move from your family of origin to your committed adult partnership, all the feelings that arose from exclusivity, closeness, and dependence rise up again. Whatever disappointment you had from yearning for something from a parent is likely to come up again with your partner. Attention? Freedom? Being known and appreciated? When your partner duplicates the failures of your parents, you'll feel it deep in your soul. You'll feel urgent about getting what you need. It's impossible to sit back and think, "Okay, so my partner doesn't value me. No problem. I'll get it from a friend."

Firefighters to the Rescue

When unworthiness, unattractiveness, disconnection, or disappointment rise up in response to your partner, it's your own Exile pain resonating from the past, followed by Firefighters leaping out to make it go away. They attack, punish, force, disconnect, and criticize to make the pain stop. Another damaging cycle has begun, and you have lost the connection and mutuality that sustain you.

In the preceding chapters, you have learned two skills that help you avoid toxic cycles: paying attention to your Exiles and giving better back. Below you will learn a third: understanding the beliefs and behaviors of Firefighters. Understanding and acknowledging Firefighters helps them relax. Then you can think clearly and make choices about how you want to respond to your partner.

Below you will hear the internal logic of the major categories of Firefighters, and see how their behavior supports their logic. You'll learn why their efforts, while well-intentioned, can never help you resolve issues with your partner.

As you read, try to focus only on your own Firefighters. If you find yourself thinking about your partner's Firefighters, remind yourself, "If it's intense, it's my own."

Angry Firefighters

Angry Firefighters have some or all of the following beliefs:

1. *You won't survive if your partner doesn't stop what he or she is doing.*

   Angry Firefighters think that being misunderstood, criticized, controlled, or disappointed will destroy you. They come out because they think you can't handle what your partner is doing. You learned in Chapter 4, "If it's intense, it's your own." Anything you think you can't tolerate is coming from an Exile. They are the ones living in your painful childhood memories, when you were too small to fight back or comfort yourself when someone hurt you.

Your angry Firefighters don't know that you can heal these hurt Exiles. They just know that there is unbearable pain, and someone has to stop it.

2. *Your partner is causing your pain.*
   Your Firefighters don't know that intense emotional pain is always your own. They blame your partner and direct their efforts to changing him or her. They are on your side, and they attack the one they think is causing the pain.

3. *You can force your partner to change.*
   Angry Firefighters believe they can force your partner to do something, such as understand you or stop criticizing you. They think the opposite of anger is giving up or submitting. They don't know that the opposite of anger is calm, clarity, connection, and confidence: saying what you mean, believing in your message, and staying clear no matter what response you get.

4. *Anger strengthens your message.*
   Angry Firefighters believe that anger makes your message stronger. Their motivation is good—to get the conversation to go somewhere, to get your partner to understand, or to get to a better place. They don't know that anger actually diminishes the power of your message and makes it easier for your partner to ignore the content. Anger may temporarily bully your partner into superficial compliance, but it won't stimulate your partner's own desire to change.

Venting Anger Is Never Effective

Anger is neither good nor bad—it just is. But when you vent your anger on your partner, it is always unproductive. You may feel immediate relief, refreshed like the air after a summer storm, ready to get back to normal. But your partner is standing there feeling as though he or she was burnt by lightning. He or she may attack back or may withdraw to recover, leaving you feeling lonely. Either way, you'll be in a toxic cycle.

Venting anger makes you lose confidence. You might feel powerful and confident while you're venting, but you're likely to lose that confidence soon after and feel depleted, hopeless, or guilty. True confidence is gentle and patient. Living without angry outbursts requires you to be confident in yourself, regardless of what is happening on the outside, and to maintain that confidence even when you are not getting what you want.

You might think anger underlines the importance of your message or strengthens its impact. Maybe you think anger will nip a situation in the bud and keep it from dragging on, or that it will get your partner's attention. But when you vent your anger, you diminish the effectiveness of your message. Your partner will be more concerned with defending him- or herself than with your meaning.

However productive the motive of angry parts, the result is synergistically disastrous, as your Firefighters trigger your partner's Firefighters, fueling a toxic loop from protector to protector. It can take days or weeks to get back to connection and intimacy.

What Angry Parts Think

Here are some of things you may hear yourself thinking when your angry parts are controlling you. Remember, we're not talking about what your partner is doing to make you angry, but your own reasons for anger. To get benefit from this exercise, you will have to shift away from blaming your anger on your partner's behavior.

Check off familiar thoughts below.

_____ I have to be angry and force change because it's unbearable when you don't (wash the dishes, give me more/less sex, respect my needs, appreciate me, etc.).

_____ I have to be angry or you won't get the importance of my message.

_____ I have to be angry or you'll ignore me.

___ I have to be angry so you will change and we can save our relationship.

___ I have to be angry or else I won't be strong.

___ I have to be angry or I'll feel invisible.

___ I have to be angry because I can't stand not being in control.

___ I have to be angry because the only way to deal with conflict is to bully people.

___ I have to be angry or you won't hear me.

___ I have to be angry or you will control me.

___ I have to be angry because it's my only hope for change.

___ I have to be angry or I won't get what I need.

Or add your own:

_____

_____

_____

Contemptuous Firefighters

Contempt communicates to the recipient that he or she is a worthless, inferior human being. It destroys the person's goodness. Contempt is a momentary attempt to destroy someone in the service of getting a point across. These may sound like strong words, but they describe why contempt is so antithetical to intimacy (Gottman, 1999).

Let's listen to the thoughts of contemptuous Firefighters. Check off the ones you recognize.

___ You are a bad person.

___ You are stupid.

___ There is something wrong with you.

Or add your own:

_____

_____

Arguing Firefighters

Have you ever noticed that disagreeing with your partner can sometimes be fun, playful, and stimulating, and other times it can leave you feeling disconnected and unsatisfied?

When arguing Firefighters take over, they try to prove your partner wrong. They believe that explaining why you disagree will influence your partner and make him or her treat you better. They replace a relaxed exchange of ideas with a driven, forcing need to make him or her see your point of view. They say, "Yeah, but," after listening to a sentence or two, or interrupt so they won't miss their turn or lose the chance to make their point.

Arguing Firefighters don't realize that if your partner isn't listening, he or she is already involved in a system of protection and guardedness. Explaining and interrupting won't change that.

Your partner won't change because you have argued a point. Paradoxically, change is more likely if he or she feels heard and understood. When you argue, no one wins and the conversation stalemates.

Check off familiar thoughts below.

___ I can't listen to you until you listen to me.
___ You're wrong. My point is the correct one.
___ I can't listen to you if you don't see my point of view.
___ I have to set the facts right before I can listen to you.

Or add your own:

_____

_____

_____

Distancing Firefighters

Distancing Firefighters whisk you away when they think you are being hurt. They want you to go off in a huff to sulk by yourself or lose yourself in other activities. They identify the most obvious source of the hurt (your partner) and get you away from him or her. They want to convince you that being cold and distant, sleeping alone, or living day to day without connection is your best solution. They don't think about your loneliness, and they are not aware that there could be a creative outcome.

Distancing Firefighters may carry you away to workaholism, over-involvement with children, or to affairs. Sometimes they cut off awareness so completely that you're dissociated—you don't feel, see, or hear what's in front of you.

Distancing Firefighters blame your partner for the distance. They say to you, "She's making you distant. It's her fault. If she would (reach out to you, care about you, listen to you), you wouldn't have to be distant." These Firefighters don't know that you can make a choice to leave a situation without blaming or shaming your partner.

Distancing doesn't help. When you return to your partner, nothing has changed. There hasn't been productive engagement on the issues that made you distance in the first place. In addition, when you distance, you take your pain with you so that your partner can't see it and feel remorse for what he or she did.

Check off familiar thoughts below.

___ I have to distance because I cannot bear the feeling of intrusion.

___ I have to distance because I can't tolerate how depressed you get when I say how I feel.

___ I have to distance to avoid getting too angry.

___ I have to distance because there is no hope for change.

___ I have to distance because I can't stand the feeling of conflict.

___ I have to distance because if I said how I felt, you would feel crushed, and I would feel guilty and responsible.

Or add your own:

_____

_____

Hopeless and Resigned Firefighters

Hopeless and resigned Firefighters sedate you into a dull, safe state so that you aren't overwhelmed or crushed by disappointment. People may judge you when you are hopeless, not understanding that it is often just another Firefighter trying to help you carry out your daily tasks and manage your life.

Resigned Firefighters help you stay in relationships. They say to you, "You have big problems and you can't fix them. You can't leave the relationship, so you should resign yourself." You find yourself settling for a dull commitment to longevity rather than trying something new. Sometimes resignation or hopelessness takes over after anger has run its course.

Hopeless Firefighters provide an antidote to alternating between hope and disappointment. They think it's better to give up and not care because it hurts too much to try and be disappointed once again. They lack faith in your creativity and ability to respond.

Resigned and hopeless Firefighters don't know that unforeseen solutions can arise. There are many reasons for hopelessness, but none make sense if you trust your confidence and creativity in the face of change.

Check off familiar thoughts below.

___ I'll feel safe and I won't do anything rash if I'm hopeless.

___ If I stop hoping, I won't have to be so disappointed when I don't get what I want.

___ I am hopeless about change, so it's better to give up.

___ This relationship is unworkable, and I don't trust myself to leave, so it's better to resign myself to it.

___ I think you are causing our problems, and you won't change, so I have to be hopeless.

Or add your own:

_____

_____

Righteous, Moralizing Firefighters

It's rare to meet a couple without meeting righteous, moralizing Firefighters. Sooner or later one or the other will communicate, "It's wrong to (yell, criticize, ignore) me. Civilized (mature, desirable, intelligent) people don't do that." These kinds of Firefighters are different from criticism—and just as destructive.

You cannot stay connected and be moralistic. Delivering moralistic judgments separates you from your partner and prevents you from keeping your heart open. Moralizing keeps you from feeling how painful it is to be criticized, judged, or ignored.

Moralizing doesn't work because your partner won't be touched by your experience unless you show how hurt you are. He or she won't accept your influence (Gottman, 1999) if you are not connected. In addition, you won't feel peace inside unless you encounter the reality of your pain.

The most powerful feedback you can give your partner is to show how hurt you are by his or her behavior. This doesn't mean collapsing into hopelessness or settling into a feeling of victimization, but just showing what you feel.

Check off familiar thoughts below.

_____ I am going to explain why your behavior is wrong.
_____ That is not the right way to treat me or anyone else.
_____ You shouldn't (criticize, yell, punish, distance).
_____ I know what's right and you should do it.

Or add your own:

_____

_____

Lecturing Firefighters

Lecturing Firefighters notice that you don't like things your partner does, and they want to help by talking at your partner and telling him or her what to think or do. They rise up a notch above your partner, thinking they have greater wisdom or knowledge. People often lecture with a neutral, logical tone, thinking they are being rational and clear. They might not realize that they are acting superior and alienating their partner.

When you are sure you know what your partner should do, you leave mutuality and curiosity behind. You lose the opportunity to let your partner surprise you with what he or she knows.

Lecturing Firefighters sometimes try to help when your partner is arguing, criticizing, or distancing. But that's when your partner's Firefighters have already taken over and identified you as the problem. If you are the problem, you cannot be the teacher.

You are more likely to communicate a point to your partner when you are speaking from your own experience, as an equal, than when you lecture your partner. You will learn more about communicating your beliefs effectively, and what to do when your partner rejects them, in Chapter 10, *Feedback: The Other Side of the Coin*.

Check off familiar thoughts below.

___ You should listen to me because I have more knowledge.
___ If you would only listen to me, you would understand what you are doing wrong.

Or add your own:

_____

_____

Punishing Firefighters

Punishing Firefighters want to teach your partner a lesson by hurting him or her. They can be cold, logical, or mocking. Sometimes they try to hurt your partner the same way your partner is hurting you, hoping that will make your partner change. Punishing Firefighters don't know that you can express your feelings clearly and directly. They don't know that you can tolerate a gap in time before your partner understands what you are saying, and that you have the

capacity to find other solutions while you are waiting.
Check off familiar thoughts below.

__ I have to punish you so you will understand how much
you hurt me.
__ I have to punish you because you did something bad.
__ I'm leaving the room or sleeping on the couch to
punish you.
__ You are going to miss me and realize you did something bad.

Or add your own:

_____
_____

Addictive Firefighters

Firefighters often use addictions to stop pain. They access a whole
range of behaviors, from socially acceptable to illegal and deadly.
Perhaps they steer you to eat until you're uncomfortable, shop till
you drop, work late every night, retreat into sports, drink alcohol,
use drugs, gamble too much, or get consumed by pornography.
Whatever the method, the purpose is to divert you from pain.
Addictive Firefighters don't think you can handle what you are
feeling, and they whisk you away from it.
Check off familiar thoughts below.

__ I need to drink or use drugs to relax in this relationship.
__ I need pornography when I'm upset with my partner,
even though I feel bad afterward.
__ I'll feel relief if I eat some more even though I'm already full.
__ Shopping takes my mind off things.

Or add your own:

_____
_____

Self-Harming Firefighters

Some Firefighters hurt the body so emotional pain will stop. Perhaps they make a little cut in the skin, or pull out hair, or apply something hot. With all attention focused on the resulting physical pain, emotional pain recedes.

Suicidal thoughts belong in this category. They come from Firefighters who have a backup plan for relief if all else fails and you can't get out of your pain. They might comfort with the thought, "If you die, you won't hurt anymore."

If you know these Firefighters are trying to help, you won't judge or fear them, and you can be curious and compassionate when you or someone else thinks about suicide. Paradoxically, the more understanding you are, the more persuasive you will be when you try to dissuade someone from killing him- or herself. Suicidal Firefighters, like all Firefighters, appreciate understanding. If you can stay calm when someone talks about suicide, be curious about the reason, and offer understanding, you will be more effective at helping the person give up his or her plans, or at least postpone them until he or she can get help.

Professionals have the power to send suicidal patients to the hospital, and anyone can and should call the police when they think someone is at risk of self-harm. But you cannot force someone to live. In the long run, understanding will be more effective than temporary restrictive measures.

Forcing Your Partner to Change

You may have noticed that many of the Firefighters described above are trying to force someone to do something. Let's look at the experience of forcing in more depth.

Firefighters force because they think you cannot bear what your partner is doing. They think you are a child, lacking inner resources to stay calm and confident when you are being criticized, ignored, or controlled. Therefore, they must rescue you by forcing your partner to change. They do not realize that you are no longer a child and that you have access to all of the resources you need.

Firefighters don't know that you can find the Exile behind an unbearable experience (as you did in Exercise 6), form a relationship with it, and help it let go of the pain of the past. Then you'll be able to say to yourself, "It hurts when my partner rejects me, but I can manage it. I can speak up for my experience."

Forcing is not a loving thing to do. When you try to force people to change, you communicate that you don't accept them as they are. Love without acceptance is not a full, satisfying love to give or receive. It leaves you knotted, tense, and limited in your loving, and it feels incomplete to the other person.

Forcing is an act of aggression against the autonomy of another person. People have free will. They are not objects designed to meet others' needs. If you respect your partner's autonomy, you will understand that he or she needs to change voluntarily, not through force.

Forcing may feel powerful in the moment, but it is not effective in the long run. Eventually, a person who feels forced will be resentful or rebellious.

When you give up forcing and begin to express yourself with calm and compassionate connection, surprising opportunities open up. You may find your partner receptive to your feedback for the first time. You may see things in your partner that you never noticed before.

If you decide you truly cannot bear your partner's behavior, it may be better to leave than to try to force him or her to change. You'll be able to exit peacefully, knowing that you respected your partner even though you couldn't tolerate his or her behavior.

Check off familiar thoughts below.

____ I have to make you to listen to me.
____ I have to force you to be more intimate with me.
____ I have to force you to accept my solution.
____ I have to make you tell me what you really mean.
____ I have to make you use the right words to talk to me.
____ I have to make you talk to me about your feelings.
____ I have to make you agree to my plan.

___ I have to make you stop criticizing me.

___ I have to make you change so I'll feel immediate relief.

Or add your own:

_____

_____

Firefighters Put You on the Express Train

Have you ever gotten on an express train by mistake? You get on and you whiz past station after station, unable to get off. You're going fast, but not where you want to go.

Firefighters put you on an express train. They conclude that your partner is responsible for hurting you, that you can't bear it, and that the pain has to stop as soon as possible. As you ride the speeding train, you have little or no awareness of other possibilities. You focus on one thought (you're criticizing me; you don't appreciate me; you don't love me; you're trying to control me) and hurtle along a trajectory of anger, contempt, arguing, distancing, passivity, or hopelessness. You have lost the ability to get off at intermediate stops. You can't stop the momentum and be curious, compassionate, or calm.

Now that you know about angry, contemptuous, arguing, distancing, hopeless, lecturing, punishing, addictive, and self-harming Firefighters, you will recognize your own Firefighter responses more often. When you do, you can get off the express train that goes nowhere, and bring calm, clarity, curiosity, courage, creativity, confidence, and compassionate connection to your relationship, even when you feel hurt.

Now let's learn about feedback, the other side of the coin.

CHAPTER 10

Feedback: The Other Side of the Coin

Throughout this book, you have learned that if the pain you experience with your partner is intense, it's your own. Here's the other side of the coin: if the pain you experience with your partner is moderate, you can give effective feedback. When you learn to give feedback well, you will rejuvenate your relationship and prevent the staleness that comes from limiting yourself to "safe" areas of communication.

When feedback goes well, it allows you and your partner to reveal parts of yourselves that you didn't even know existed and receive surprising, enriching input from each other. The partner who gives feedback is really sharing him- or herself, and the partner who receives it has the opportunity to see him- or herself through different eyes. In the very best feedback experiences, the lines between feedback and self-revelation blur, creating a resonant, undulating music between partners. That happened one night in a session with Robert and Patricia.

Robert and Patricia had met in their forties. Robert was a classics professor who had published numerous academic articles and several lighter pieces in the *New Yorker*. Patricia spent her days as the chair of a large philanthropic organization, giving money away to worthy causes. I enjoyed sitting with them, listening to Robert's "old boy" way of talking, humorous and erudite at the same time. In his presence, I heard myself using words I didn't even know I knew. I admired Patricia's elegance, knowing it derived more from her dignity, sensitivity, and confidence than from the expensive shoes or boutique jackets she wore. They loved each other, they liked each other, and yet they felt lonely in their marriage. One night when they came in for their appointment, Patricia, normally the talkative one, invited Robert to talk. In his careful, descriptive manner, he told her that she was often drained and unhappy, and that she drank too much. Realizing that he was giving Patricia feedback, I interrupted to see if he was fully prepared for her response, whatever it might be. If he wasn't, I knew from experience that his face might redden with anger in a moment if she triggered him, or that he might give up and let her run the session.

> Mona (to Robert): How are you doing now? Are you feeling calm, connected, and confident?
>
> Robert: Yes.
>
> Mona: What could go wrong with Patricia's response? What could make you flash into anger or collapse?
>
> Robert: She'd say no, that's not true, or wave her hand (he waved his hand in the air).
>
> Mona: Can you imagine yourself staying steady, calm, and confident if she did that? Because there's no guarantee how she will respond.
>
> Robert (after a moment): Yes.
>
> Mona: Do you want to look inside and tell Patricia more about how you feel?
>
> Robert: Frustrated and impotent because you're unhappy. You drink too much and you don't see the positive. You crashed only forty-eight hours after you got back from the event in New York. You were so happy and relaxed, and then last night you were back to complaining about work, completely down.

I was alert and a little worried because I've learned that the first response to feedback is usually defensive. Like most people, Patricia responded by criticizing back.

> Patricia: You're the one who's unhappy. You complain about your colleagues and you drink, too.

After acknowledging Patricia's point of view and encouraging her to choose whether she wanted to be defensive or open, I helped Robert stay clear and communicate what it would really mean to him if Patricia weren't so unhappy and didn't drink so much.

> Mona (to Robert): What's the opposite of all that? Would you tell Patricia what she would be doing differently if this whole thing turned around?
>
> Robert: If you mastered your drinking, you'd fully enjoy one glass of wine and then stop.
>
> Mona: What would that be like for you?
>
> Robert: I would learn something. I'd be curious. I might learn how to avoid eating dessert. I would feel as though I had watched something important and be happy for Patricia. I'd be privileged to share her accomplishment. I'd have someone to share the good moments. For me, that's the opposite of lonely.
>
> Mona: Was there a time in the past when this was important to you?
>
> Robert: When my brother was playing football in 12th grade and I was in 6th grade, he told me what to expect on a date or on a job interview. He told me what to expect in college. My parents were supportive in a general way, but it was my brother who gave me advice I could really use.

I was no longer worried that Robert would get angry. His face was softly focused on the memory of his brother's caring and guidance in the midst of a disconnected family. I relaxed, because there was nothing else I needed to do. Robert had reached deep inside and revealed the personal meaning of his feedback to Patricia.

> Patricia (softening): I'm so amazed at how vulnerable you get, and I know it's hard for you. At first, I was angry. I wanted to say that I realized in New York that I don't trust you because you need me to be needy. But that's all gone now. I just feel connected and tender.

Robert was reddening with closeness instead of anger. It was clear that Patricia had listened to Robert's feedback, and she knew so much more about him than before they talked. She knew that mastering her drinking would uplift Robert and give him more confidence to deal with his own addictions, and that sharing the good moments with her reminded him of the only real experiences of warmth and engagement in his childhood—guidance from his older brother. There was a rejuvenated, enchanted feeling in the room, enveloping us all. When the session ended, I felt gratitude for the opportunity to be with people like Robert and Patricia who were willing to take such courageous chances and include me in them.

Feedback: The Risk

Feedback can be a vital and significant part of a relationship, as it was for Robert and Patricia. Your partner can give insight that comes from knowing you within the web of relatedness. You might travel to gurus or go to individual therapy for years and not get such relevant feedback. But the very fact that it's accurate is likely to make it dangerous.

Feedback is risky because it bypasses Managers' comfort zones. You may remember that Managers are in charge of limiting your behavior and your thinking on a daily basis so that nothing gets through to trigger your Exiles. They like things to stay the same, without potentially destabilizing new information. When you give feedback, you are usually trying to get your partner to be aware of something new—for example, that he or she is angry, unfocused, insensitive, or critical. Managers won't usually want this input.

If something does get through Managers' perimeters, Firefighters take over and start blaming, shaming, attacking, or distancing, trying

to diminish the discomfort within as quickly as possible. If your partner's Firefighters think that you are hurting your partner, they will
try to stop you as quickly as possible. They might use private, tender
information to hurt you and make you stop.

The deeper you see into your partner, the more accurate you
are about what you see, and the more clearly you express it, the
more likely you are to feel the storm of Firefighter reaction. Your
own Firefighters will defend you, and you'll be in a toxic blame,
attack, or distance cycle. Afterward, your own Managers, ever
vigilant to preempt pain, will tell you, "Don't go there again!" and
steer you away from giving feedback or even showing an expression
on your face that could look like feedback. You may find yourself
thinking that you should choose the safety of silence and a dull,
blind acceptance.

But the price of silence is high. If you withhold your perceptions, your relationship will stagnate. When you withhold honest
feedback, you deny your own potential to be courageous, compassionate, confident, and clear. Instead of feeling energized, you feel
distant, disappointed, or judgmental. When you hold back feedback,
you also underestimate your partner's capacity to receive feedback
and can lose respect for him or her. Learning to give feedback skillfully will help you avoid all of these dreary outcomes.

Good Feedback Has No Expectation or Need

Good feedback means saying what you notice about your partner
without expectation or need that he or she will change. Give your
feedback as if you were dropping a pebble into a tranquil pond
and watching the ripples spread out. Let go of attachment to the
results.

You can express all of what you feel and know about your
partner, but it only enhances your relationship if you respect
your partner's autonomy. Offer your clarity and perspective while
accepting your partner as he or she is. The less you try to force your
partner to change, the more chance there will be that he or she will
indeed change, perhaps in delightful, unforeseen ways.

Good Feedback Is Given with Self Qualities

You may recall the eight Self qualities. Let's go through each of them and see how they can help you give effective feedback.

Curiosity

Curiosity allows you to learn something new about your partner. You can give your feedback with clarity and confidence in your perceptions and then remain open and curious. You may find out touching, poignant things about your partner, and you will set the tone for open, fluid dialogue. If you lock yourself down and tell yourself you already know everything you need to know, feedback won't be a relaxed, happy experience for you or your partner.

Calm

Calm is often the first Self quality to fly away when partners give feedback, quickly replaced by agitation. Once that happens it's hard to gain access to any of the other Self qualities. When you can begin your feedback calmly, you will have more chance of being clear, confident, connected, creative, courageous, and curious. If you feel a sense of pressure or agitation before you start your feedback, stop. Find your calm and then begin.

Compassion

When you give feedback with compassion, you make your partner's experience as important as your own. You are willing to see into your partner's soul and experience both of you as two equally important beings. Have you ever had this experience? When I think about compassion, I think about Betty and Andrew. Often, in couples therapy sessions with me, they were attentive and caring, and they frequently connected. I knew they loved each other, but they couldn't get off their dreary merry-go-round of complaining. Andrew complained that Betty didn't listen to him, and Betty complained that Andrew didn't care about her feelings. It seemed as though they were so close to moving out of this draining pattern, but they never quite got there. One day in a session, Betty told us what happened after she took one of her Buddhist vows.

> I took my Bodhisattva vows last Sunday. It's a vow not to add to the suffering in the world. It was a beautiful ceremony. Andrew came to the reception afterward.
>
> When we got home, Andrew asked me to help him move a desk. When I didn't move it around a corner the way he wanted, his tone got nasty, like I was an idiot. It hurt so much because I was so sensitive from the ceremony. But the amazing thing was that I cared as much about him as I cared about myself. I could see that his face was dark and shut off and that he was unhappy, just as I was. I felt bad for a couple of hours, both for myself and for him. All that time, I didn't feel the slightest need for him to change or the slightest anger. I just felt the pain. Then when we got into bed, he said he was sorry. It was such a sweet moment because I hadn't been making him bad for what he did, so the apology just flowed between us and we both melted. I hope I can keep doing this.

I got calmer as Betty told her story. I felt the presence of something larger than the three of us in the room. It was compassion — caring as much for someone else's feelings as for our own.

Confidence

Confidence helps you say what you believe and stick to it when you give feedback, regardless of the response from your partner. Do you have a steady, confident feeling when you think of telling your partner what you feel? Or do you doubt your perceptions or your right to express them? If you lack confidence, you'll lose your focus when your partner objects or argues with you.

Or maybe you hold so tightly to your beliefs that you can't let your partner's response affect you. That isn't confidence either. True confidence moves freely into receptivity as you express yourself clearly and open yourself to input.

Courage

Courage helps you give feedback that your partner might not like. If you are afraid of your partner's reactions, of your own anger, or about changes that might result, you won't be able to give good feedback.

Courage helps you choose the time when you want to give feedback. Partners often put feedback off and then find themselves blurting it out impulsively. Maybe you wait until your partner does something good and then complain that he or she doesn't do it often enough. If you have the courage to listen to your perceptions and express them at a time you choose, you won't have to ruin a positive experience and discourage your partner from repeating it. It's better to convey appreciation when your partner does something you like and then wait to give your feedback later.

Sometimes partners remember their feedback when they hear the other one complaining. It might go something like this: "You think I'm critical? You're the critical one!" Piggybacking feedback doesn't work. You won't get the attention you want because your partner will be focused on his or her own ideas. Feedback is more effective when you have the courage to give it when you want to, not when someone else brings it up.

Clarity

Clarity helps you sort out your perceptions and find the words to express them. If you are confused, you will not be able to formulate your thoughts well. You might bounce from one statement to another and lose your main point. When you give feedback with clarity, your partner will be more likely to be open to the message.

If you are clear, you can go right to your main point and express it. You won't have to qualify, back up, or void your message with contradictory statements.

Connection

Your feedback is more likely to have an effect if you feel connected to your partner when you give it. Feedback without connection cannot travel to your partner's heart and awaken him or her. If you give feedback in a rational, lecturing, removed way, you will not evoke your partner's compassion and desire to participate.

Giving feedback with a feeling of connection brings you peace while you give it and a feeling of completion afterward. Giving feedback with distance or disconnection is an unsatisfying and empty experience for you. Here's how Rosa learned this.

Rosa and Peter were successful people. Peter was an architect who designed commercial buildings in New England. Rosa worked for a political organization, organizing $5,000-a-plate dinners. Much of her work involved meeting people at events and social occasions. I noticed the style and quality of her clothes and how good they looked on her, but I never got the sense that she wanted to flaunt her beauty or be better than anyone else. When she arrived after driving up and down the streets around my office looking for a parking spot, there was no sense of judgment or annoyance from her. I could see how people would want to give money to her candidate because they felt comfortable with her.

Rosa and Peter had been in couples therapy for many years. By the time they came to me, there was almost nothing left between them. "We want to work it out because of our son," they both said, conspicuously leaving out any feeling of love for each other. They argued and criticized each other constantly. They could hardly get through an event or a vacation without a blow up, often storming away from each other and returning home in different cars or even different airplanes.

In our seventh session, Rosa was telling Peter that he was unpredictable and angry. "I'm so tense when you come home. Yesterday you were so angry because you lost your keys and you snipped at me because I had dinner ready too early." Peter protested that he hadn't been angry with her, only about losing his keys. Rosa started over again and repeated the whole story, bringing in past examples of his anger, which Peter also rebutted. She was animated and oddly smiling. I was beginning to wonder when she was going to be satisfied with what she was saying.

> Mona: Are you feeling connected?
>
> Rosa (as she looked down): No.
>
> Mona: Is there a reason not to connect to Peter?

Rosa's face reddened and tears filled the corners of her eyes. I noticed that instead of seeing her skillful makeup and generic beauty, I was noticing her actual face with its unique contours. I wondered if she sometimes hid behind her makeup and clothes.

> Rosa: I'm scared. I'm scared to tell Peter how angry he is.
>
> Rosa (looking up and gazing directly at Peter, still tearful): You are so angry. I never know what to expect from you.

She stopped, not needing to repeat herself. Peter was looking directly at her without a word of argument. Her words were the same, but now she was connected when she said them.

At the end of the session, I asked Rosa what she liked about the way she communicated. She answered, "I connected with myself, and then I was able to connect with Peter." Peter was relaxed, saying at the end of the session, "I liked visiting with Rosa."

They had many months of couples therapy ahead. Sometimes we didn't know if we were meeting so they could find a way to be happy together or to separate with calm and mutual respect. Either way, communication with connection was the only way they could move forward.

If, like Rosa, you give feedback with connection, you will be more satisfied with yourself. You won't have to repeat yourself. You can sit back and notice how your partner responds, knowing you have done your best.

Creativity

When you are creative, new ideas and ways to express yourself come about easily. You'll be able to notice your partner or things happening around you, and use them playfully to express yourself. Something unexpected may happen—you may make a joke that's funnier than usual or find yourself improvising in a way you could never have imagined before. When you are creative, feedback can be a fun, lighthearted experience as well as a deep one. When creativity is present, delight and surprise will appear in the most unexpected places.

What Gets in the Way of Self Qualities

Self qualities will help you give effective feedback. If any of them are missing, you may quickly lose your focus or find yourself arguing or collapsing within seconds. Let's look at some things that might get in the way of Self qualities. You might think of these things as parts or as feelings within you.

Fear

If courage or confidence is missing, some of your parts might be afraid of what will happen when you give your feedback. If they are, you might lose yourself and collapse if your partner doesn't respond well. Do any of these thoughts feel familiar?

- ___ My partner can get so angry. I will feel totally crushed.
- ___ My partner can be so shaming when she thinks I'm being critical. I would feel so crushed.
- ___ I'll just curl up and retreat if she dismisses me.
- ___ I'm afraid of feeling controlled.
- ___ I feel horrible if he doesn't hear me.
- ___ I'll crumble if he criticizes me instead of listening.
- ___ I'll get too angry if she doesn't hear me. I better not say anything because I don't trust myself to stay calm.
- ___ I'm afraid of what could happen if I'm truthful.

—— It's always been safer to hold back.

—— Things get worse when I speak up.

—— If I criticize her, she'll shame me. She is so good at turning it back on me. I can't bear the shame.

If your parts are afraid of something, listen to them. They might be basing their fears on childhood experiences. As an adult, you don't have to collapse in the face of emotional attack. Unless you are in an abusive situation, you can stay present even if you get a negative response to your feedback. You can't give good feedback until you reassure those parts that you will be okay even if you get the worst response.

Guilt

Do you feel guilty after you give feedback? Do you have parts that think you will hurt your partner by giving him or her feedback? Perhaps you have a belief that you should be nurturing all the time and that you are bad if you are assertive. Listen inside and see if you hear anything like this?

—— It's bad to say what I think. I should be satisfied with what I have.

—— I am bad if I need something.

—— Asking for what I want is being harsh.

—— I can't help feeling as though it's my fault if she feels upset.

Paradoxically, you hurt your partner less when you give direct feedback. If you wait and your Firefighters come out to do it for you, they won't be kind.

Abandonment

Perhaps you fear that your partner will withdraw or leave you if you give feedback. Do you hear anything like this?

—— If I speak up, he'll want to leave me. I don't trust myself to adjust to that.

—— He might get depressed if I really say what I mean. I can't stand how lonely it feels when he goes away.

If you hear these things, these are your young Exiles. It's true, children can't bear abandonment, but you are no longer a child. Your parts need acknowledgment of their fears and reassurance that you can handle loneliness. You can tell them that you will be lonelier if you don't speak up.

Exercise 10: Before You Give Feedback, Part 1

Before you give feedback, scan yourself for Self qualities. In the following list, check the ones that are missing.

Curiosity

—— Do I feel curious and interested in my partner's experience, or am I only interested in my own?

Calm

—— Am I calm, or do I feel agitated? Do I need my partner to change in order to feel calm, or can I feel calm no matter what happens?

Compassion

—— Am I analyzing my partner from a superior position, or am I sharing from one equal to another? Do I feel compassion, or am I judging my partner? Do I care about my partner's feelings as much as my own, or am I immersed in my own pain?

Confidence

—— Am I feeling confident, or am I questioning myself?

Courage

—— Do I have the courage to express myself, or am I frightened by what might happen?

Clarity

___ Am I feeling clear about my perceptions, or am I vacillating or confused?

Connection

___ Am I feeling connected to my partner, or do I feel distant and disconnected?

Creativity

___ Do I have a feeling of lightness and creativity so that I might surprise myself with new ways to communicate, or do I feel dull and locked into one way of communicating?

If any Self qualities are missing, list them in the next exercise and follow the instructions. You will be looking for scared or hurt feelings coming from an Exile that lives in the past. You will have an opportunity to connect with the Exile and its feelings, acknowledge its reality, help it relax, and see if the Self quality returns.

1. Missing Self quality: _____

a. Look for an Exile that is scared or hurt. Do you see it, feel it, or hear its words? Write how you perceive your Exile:

_____

_____

_____

_____

_____

b. Connect with your Exile. Acknowledge its reality. Listen to its beliefs. Let it know you are there. Assure it that you have resources now that you didn't have before.

_____

_____

_____

_____

c. Does the missing Self quality return? How does it feel? Can
    you imagine yourself giving feedback with the Self quality
    present? What would it be like?

_____

_____

_____

_____

_____

2. Missing Self quality: _____

a. Look for an Exile that is scared or hurt. Do you see it, feel it,
    or hear its words? Write how you perceive your Exile:

_____

_____

_____

_____

_____

b. Connect with your Exile. Acknowledge its reality. Listen to its
    beliefs. Let it know you are there. Assure it that you have re-
    sources now that you didn't have before.

_____

_____

_____

_____

_____

c. Does the missing Self quality return? How does it feel? Can
    you imagine yourself giving feedback with the Self quality
    present? What would it be like?

_____

_____

_____

_____

3. Missing Self quality: _____

a. Look for an Exile that is scared or hurt. Do you see it, feel it, or hear its words? Write how you perceive your Exile:

_____

_____

_____

_____

_____

_____

b. Connect with your Exile. Acknowledge its reality. Listen to its beliefs. Let it know you are there. Assure it that you have resources now that you didn't have before.

_____

_____

_____

_____

_____

_____

c. Does the missing Self quality return? How does it feel? Can you imagine yourself giving feedback with the Self quality present? What would it be like?

_____

_____

_____

_____

_____

_____

Extra Caution: Don't Start Yet!

You've done your preparatory work, but don't start giving feedback yet. Getting ready for your partner's response after you give feedback is at least as important as preparing yourself. This might sound like a lot of work, but it takes far less effort than dealing with anger, argument, or distance after feedback has gone awry.

Remember, your partner's Managers don't want to hear anything new. They spend their time guarding a safe perimeter, trying to create a stable sense of goodness and capability, trying to keep anything away that triggers Exiles. They don't know that accepting feedback from you is enriching. Your partner's Firefighters are ready to attack, argue, or distance to make the feedback go away.

After you give feedback, you are likely to get several waves of negative, protective responses from your partner. The last wave is likely to be the most challenging as your partner brings out the big guns to stop the pain he or she has (wrongly) decided you are causing. Since your partner knows you so well, he or she knows what will hurt you the most. That's what your partner will use for the third wave. Be prepared to get something back that will startle you, hurt you, and destabilize you. You may find yourself thinking, "She could have said anything but that. That is the most unfair, hurtful thing I have ever heard."

Maybe you think this is overly negative and you recall times your partner has responded well to feedback. That's great, but it's better to prepare for the worst. What have you got to lose? You'll get the chance to examine yourself, allow more Self qualities to shine, and be prepared in case your partner's reaction is challenging. And you can consider giving riskier, deeper feedback if you are confident and well prepared.

Sometimes your partner's first response is reasonable and gratifying. You'll think to yourself, "He gets it! He respects my input, and he's going to change." Beware of what comes next. If it's something negative, you could be especially devastated when you fall from the good feeling of acknowledgment to the bad feeling of attack or abandonment.

Exercise 11: Before You Give Feedback, Part 2

1. What feedback do you most want to give your partner? What observation would you like to share?

   _____

   _____

   _____

   _____

   _____

2. Imagine yourself giving this feedback. List your partner's most likely first response (You do that too, I haven't done that lately, Why are you so critical, etc.).

   _____

   _____

   _____

   _____

   _____

3. What Self quality might you lose when your partner gives his or her most likely first response? Here's the list:

   ___ Curiosity   ___ Courage

   ___ Calm   ___ Clarity

   ___ Compassion   ___ Connection

   ___ Confidence   ___ Creativity

4. What might happen when you lose these qualities? Would any of your Firefighters come out?

   _____

   _____

   _____

   _____

   _____

5. See if you can find the Exile behind the Firefighter. Meet it, acknowledge it, and see if it can relax. Imagine maintaining your Self qualities even if your partner gives the response you listed.

_____
_____
_____
_____

6. Imagine your partner's second protective response (you don't love me, you want someone else, you're never satisfied). What Self quality might you lose when your partner responds this way? Check the ones that are missing.

____ Curiosity   ____ Courage
____ Calm   ____ Clarity
____ Compassion   ____ Connection
____ Confidence   ____ Creativity

7. What might happen when you lose these Self qualities? Would any of your Firefighters come out?

_____
_____
_____
_____

8. See if you can find the Exile (or feeling) behind the Firefighter. Meet it, acknowledge it, and see if it can relax. Imagine maintaining your Self qualities even if your partner sends his or her second wave of protective responses.

_____
_____
_____
_____

9. Now imagine your partner's third response. What is the worst response he or she is likely to give? What response would hurt you the most (rage, depression, withdrawal, coldness)? What Self quality might you lose when your partner responds this way? Here's the list:

___ Curiosity   ___ Courage

___ Calm   ___ Clarity

___ Compassion   ___ Connection

___ Confidence   ___ Creativity

10. What might happen when you lose these Self qualities? Would any of your Firefighters come out?

_____

_____

_____

_____

_____

11. See if you can find the Exile (or feeling) behind the Firefighter. Meet it, acknowledge it, and see if it can relax. Imagine maintaining your Self qualities even if your partner sends his or her third wave.

_____

_____

_____

_____

_____

Now you're ready to give feedback. You may find it a thrilling, challenging, rewarding experience that leaves you more confident in yourself, more present in the relationship, and closer to your partner. Feedback can make your relationship a rich, surprising place in which you and your partner reveal your deepest natures and experience mutual influence.

Couples do two things in my office: become aware of their own intense reactions and give feedback. Now you know how to do both. Choose one and be aware of which one you are choosing.

CHAPTER 11

Three Things That Work in a Fight

Y ou are in a fight. Your Firefighters are engaged and doing what they do best: arguing, attacking, shaming, teaching, directing, pushing, and disconnecting. They are ready to take you away from the relationship and offer you the solace of solitude, the refuge of addictions, and the angry righteousness of a hardened heart.

Your partner's Firefighters are also engaged. Together, they are causing a lot of damage, and when it's over, you'll feel lonely. Sometimes it can take days, weeks, or months to reconnect. No one wants to be so alone, but sometimes it seems as if there is no way to avoid it.

Have you tried to end a fight once it's started? Then you probably found out it's hard to stop the momentum. When Firefighters are on the job, it's hard to reason. Humor is met with suspicion and you can hardly get one sentence out without getting attacked.

Here's some good news: there are three things that do work in a fight:

1. The Do Over
2. 100% Admitting
3. Giving Better Back

These three things work because they disarm Firefighters. They don't ask anything of your partner, and they don't criticize. Under these conditions, Firefighters have nothing to protect. They relax and you can get back to connection, communication, and fun.

The Do Over

The Do Over is about what you could have done differently at some point in the fight. It's only about you and your actions. The Do Over is one of those topsy-turvy approaches that doesn't make any sense at first. You are probably more focused on what your partner could have done differently than on your own actions. For the Do Over to work, you have to let all those things go and focus on what you could have done differently, even if seems so tiny compared to what your partner did.

Here's how it works:

1. Ask permission to do a Do Over. Make sure your partner understands it's only about what you did and nothing about what he/she did. If your partner says no, wait patiently until later.

2. Describe the moment in the disagreement when you think you could have done something differently.

3. Do your Do Over in the present tense, as if you were back in time at that very moment.

4. Be ready for your partner to respond poorly.

Why should you be ready for your partner to respond poorly? His or her Firefighters are engaged, and their job is to look for reasons to attack. They will probably interpret your Do Over as some kind of attack and respond accordingly.

That doesn't mean your Do Over is a failure. You just have to be prepared to wait awhile for your partner to calm down. Most likely, your partner will reciprocate with something very nice. Maybe it will be something related to the fight, or maybe it will be something completely unexpected. Be on the watch. You might not get exactly what you want, but if you can appreciate what you do get, you will be supporting a return to happiness and connection.

If you do Do Overs a lot, you may find that your partner calms down more quickly. He or she may come to trust your efforts and maybe even try it themselves.

I taught a workshop on IFS couples therapy at one of the IFS annual conferences, including a role play demonstration of the Do Over. Several days later I got this email from Ana, one of the participants:

> I had the pleasure of attending your workshop on couples therapy at the recent IFS conference. The next day I had a sweet and humbling encounter with my husband.
>
> The day after I learned about the "Do Over" from you, I was talking to my husband Steve on the phone. "Steve," I said, "Would you take a thank you gift to the Murphys down the street? They took care of the cats while we were on vacation." I knew this would be excruciating for him. He groaned and growled and said, "Well, thanks for calling," and hung up. At first, my part that needs him to be perfect popped up and said in my head, "It's the least he could do. After all, I picked the gift out, bought it, carried it home from France, and wrapped it!" Self was able to jump in pretty quickly and I thought about what I had learned in your workshop the day before. Then we texted back and forth.
>
> Me: Hi again. Remember when I asked you to take the present to the Murphys? I'd like to do that over.
>
> Him: OK.

Me: I know doing things like that is uncomfortable for you. I'll be happy to take it to her when I get home.

Him: Really?

Me: Yes

Him: Did you learn that at your conference today?

Me: No, yesterday. It's called a Do-over. You likie?

Him: No, me LOVIE! I want to learn it too. :)

I felt so much closer to him after the do-over and I felt much better about myself as well.

If you try the Do Over, you will also feel better about yourself. You'll have the confidence from knowing you are not caught up in your parts, and you are being who you really are. You will feel the warm glow of generosity, knowing you gave something when you wanted to get something. Like Ana, you may also experience surprising, delightful results.

100% Admitting

100% Admitting is a lot like the Do Over. It's all about you. It leaves out anything and everything your partner did wrong. There is no but, because, or if only. It's just you admitting something you did that started the fight or made it worse.

Again, don't expect immediate results. Do your 100% Admitting, listen to what your partner says, and don't engage in any negativity at all. Even if it seems like your partner doesn't get it, forego the temptation to argue. Simply do your 100%, listen with connection and calm, and wait for your partner to calm down.

Here's an example:

Andrew and Lydia came in saying they had a good week. Andrew was proud that he had kept the agreement he had made. First thing every morning, he resisted his iPhone and turned to give Lydia his attention. His face was open and happy, and he was glowing with his achievement. Lydia was somewhere else. She complained, "There's always something wrong with me. You think I'm stupid and inadequate. You shift to out-of-work mode for others, but not for me."

Andrew's face fell. His eyes were dull and he was looking down. I waited to see what Lydia would do. I had learned to expect quick, brilliant changes from her.

"I'm so self-absorbed in my own problems and it's not him making me feel good. I'm so stressed out getting back to work. I'm not acting right."

Andrew brightened up immediately. She had done it. She shifted out of her complaints to 100% admitting. She admitted something about herself, left him completely out of it, and stopped talking.

Giving Better Back

Giving Better Back is the third thing that works in a fight. Like the Do Over and 100% Admitting, it's all about you, doesn't criticize or demand anything from your partner, and isn't threatening to Firefighters. The steps to Giving Better Back are detailed in Chapter 6. You give better energy than you are getting. You could also think of giving what you wish you were getting. Be careful not to interpret this as being nice. Sometimes "better" is clear, assertive, confident, and direct.

CHAPTER 12
Take the 30 Day Challenge

You've learned a lot. You have found the golden key to keeping your love vibrant and alive: If it's intense, it's your own. You know that if you have an intensely unhappy reaction to your mate, it's yours. It comes from you and you are the only one who can handle it.

You learned that your defensive, angry, and distancing reactions to your partner are your Firefighters protecting your Exiles from further hurt. You've learned that the best way to deal with your Firefighters is to acknowledge and love them. No longer do you have to avoid, judge, or fight your own reactions.

You've met the hurt little boys and girls who are being protected, and you've let them know you are there with them.

You've found out the joy of taking responsibility for your own actions and the beauty of the love that arises between you and your partner when you do this. You can even give feedback and remain calm and connected when it doesn't go over well at first.

Would you like to take it to the next level?

Take the 30 day challenge. Challenge yourself to change something for 30 days in a row.

You'll be putting your learning into action and doing it for 30 days in a row. The steady repetition for 30 days will build confidence and become habitual.

What behavior do you want to change? Perhaps you'd like to eliminate sarcasm, anger, or criticism toward your partner. That could be your 30 day challenge. You could set your goals for 30 days without sarcasm, anger, or criticism toward your mate. Every day that you can express yourself without the behavior you target is a success.

Or perhaps you'd like to change your thinking. Your goal could be to stay aware of your own internal reactions and to remember "If it's intense, it's my own." Whenever intense disturbance replaces your calm, connected, clear presence, you own it as your own reaction. You turn your focus away from blaming your partner to attending to yourself.

We're talking about positive change here, but as you've learned in this book, the best way to make positive changes is to look with compassion and love at what's in the way. And that's exactly what you will be doing in the 30 day challenge.

Are you ready?

Here it is! It starts on the next page so you can print it out and use the daily log pages.

The first thing you will do is set your intention. If you choose to change your thinking, it might sound like this:

I commit to looking at myself when I am intensely upset with my partner. Whenever I have lost connection, calm, clarity, courage, compassion, curiosity, confidence or creativity, it will be about me only. If my reactions to my mate are intensely disturbing, I will look at them as my own. I commit to doing this 30 days in a row. If and when I miss a day, I will start over at Day 1.

If you choose to change a behavior, it might sound like this:

I commit to eliminating criticism toward my partner.
I commit to eliminating attack toward my partner.
I commit to eliminating shame and blame toward my partner.

I commit to appreciating my partner much more than I criticize him or her.

I commit to being direct when I want something, and eliminating passive-aggressive behavior.

It's your 30 days. Pick something that means something to you.

Note: If you need some extra help along the way, Internal Family Systems therapists are in almost every state, and if you don't want to go into an office, they are only a phone call away. Go to www.selfleadership.org to find one. Please read the disclaimer on the back of the title page of this book so you will understand that this exercise is not offered as psychological advice.

30 Day Challenge
If it's intense, it's my own

My intention: _____

_____

_____

_____

_____

_____

_____

My start date: _____

Why I am doing this (keep adding reasons to this as you go along):

_____

_____

_____

_____

_____

_____

_____

_____

_____

_____

_____

_____

Daily Log

Date _____   Day number _____

What my partner was doing when I was tempted to: (fill in the behavior you want to eliminate)

_____

_____

Did my Firefighters come up? If you check one or more statements below, it was probably a Firefighter.

_____I didn't care about my partner's feelings
_____I was agitated
_____I was not connected
_____I was shaming/blaming
_____I was forcing my partner to do or stop doing something

What was my Firefighter protecting?

_____

_____

Appreciation for my Firefighter (thank you for being willing to protect me, you are so skilled at _____, thank you for letting me handle this, thank you for letting me try it another way, etc.).

_____

_____

Connect with the Exile your Firefighter was protecting. Sit with it, write a letter to it, breathe into it, and listen to it.

_____

_____

Things that surprised me, made me proud, or brought me joy and happiness.

_____

_____

CHAPTER 13

What to Expect in IFS Couples Therapy

opefully the ideas and exercises in this book have been helpful to you, and you feel confident that you can improve your relationship. Or perhaps you feel that you and your partner could use some professional help. This chapter will tell you what to expect from a couples therapist who uses the IFS model. Since there are so many IFS therapists in the United States and in other countries, there is a lot of variety in the way IFS is practiced. This chapter gives the basics of the IFS approach.

Discover Your Own Abilities to Solve Your Problems

Since everyone has Self qualities available to them (curiosity, calm, compassion, confidence, courage, clarity, connection, and creativity), there is no need for IFS couples therapists to teach you these things. When they see something missing in your relationship, they look for the Managers and Firefighters that are obscuring your natural abilities.

Partnerships are better when contempt is absent, there is more appreciation than criticism, problem solving is done with connection and humor, and partners accept influence from each other (Gottman, 1999). But IFS couples therapists don't usually teach these skills. Instead, they ask questions about what's in the way. Are there reasons to criticize, disconnect, or reject input? Maybe you'll find out you have parts that believe that criticizing is the best way to get your partner to change, that accepting influence means losing control, or that distance is safer than engagement. Once you understand the logic behind unproductive behavior, your natural couples skills will emerge. You'll find yourself being spontaneously gentle, creative, open, appreciative, and assertive. When you formulate your own plan to change, it will be more specific, elegant, and productive than anything a couples therapist could have suggested.

IFS couples therapists want to collaborate with you to find solutions. They are respectful of your own abilities and do not present themselves as experts who know the answer to your problems. In fact, you will probably find that your IFS couples therapist is willing to be wrong and happy to be corrected or re-directed. The answers lie within you, and your IFS couples therapist has the skills to help you find them.

No Need to Label You or Your Partner as Psychologically Damaged

IFS therapists do not try to figure out how your early environment damaged you. Rather, they focus on getting to know Managers that developed extreme behaviors to help you adapt. For example, IFS therapists wouldn't usually say, "You are mistrustful because your early family interactions were too unpredictable." Instead, they would say, "Would you like to get to know the part of you that is mistrustful? How do you feel toward it? Would you like to understand it better? Would you like to ask it what would happen if it weren't so mistrustful?" By answering these questions, you will find out if you have a part that is trying to protect you by being mistrustful, and if there is an Exile within you that was hurt, for example, by unpredictable behavior. Instead of "How can I help this person develop more trust?" an IFS therapist thinks, "How can I help this person understand and validate her mistrusting part?"

IFS therapists see problematic behavioral patterns as the well-intentioned work of Managers and Firefighters trying to do the best they can under difficult circumstances. With the presence of Self energy, you can get to know these protective parts and help them relax. The solutions that arise from Self-part relationships will be far superior to anything you could have imagined beforehand.

No Judgment

IFS couples therapists accept both partners unconditionally, no matter how they act in their worst moments. Instead of judgment, there will be curiosity and compassion. IFS couples therapists know that extreme behaviors result from Managers and Firefighters trying to do their jobs, not from innate badness or character flaws.

IFS couples therapists will not usually see one partner as the victim and the other as the perpetrator (remember, we are not talking about physically or emotionally abusive situations). Even though it might look as though one partner is controlling or demeaning, the other might have parts that think they need to accept victimization. For instance, are there parts that think they deserve bad treatment, feel helpless, or feel frightened? Once such parts have the opportunity to relax, partners who seemed like victims will find new resources to respond assertively.

Perhaps you think the first thing a couples therapist should do is to tell your partner not to be so critical, angry, selfish, controlling, or distant. That might be tempting for the couples therapist, but taking an educational approach usually doesn't solve couples' problems because those critical, angry, selfish, controlling, or distant behaviors come from Managers and Firefighters that are just trying to help. They need acknowledgment and understanding for their efforts, not rebuke. A curious attitude toward protective parts is much more effective than arguing with them. You'll learn that curiosity about your partner's protective parts is much more effective than fighting with them.

IFS advocates respect for the effort, dedication, and caring that underlie Managers' and Firefighters' efforts. These parts need understanding before they can leave their restrictive roles and embrace a fuller existence. You will be amazed at the possibilities that arise when you are able to let Managers and Firefighters speak for their beliefs and when you hear the poignant reasons behind their efforts.

Would You Like to Speak for That Part?

You may hear your IFS couples therapist asking you to speak for a part instead of from it. You may recall how Sarah learned to speak for her angry and hurt parts in Chapter 2. She said to her husband John, "I get scared when you take your eyes off the road. It feels like you aren't taking enough care of me, and it brings back memories for me. It was what I was trying to say when I was angry, but now I could say it straight." She was truthful and descriptive of her experience, but not immersed in it.

If you are speaking from a part, you will often have a claustrophobic, stuffy experience. You may feel limited to one point of view and reality, as though you were living in a big house but locked in just one room. Then you might find yourself switching to another part, with different beliefs and worldviews, but just as restricted. When you speak for a part, you express the same beliefs and experience, but in a fluid and spacious way.

IFS couples therapists will welcome every experience you have but will encourage you to unblend and communicate with a sense of spaciousness. When this happens, you will have a better experience, and your partner will be more likely to comprehend what you are saying.

What's Happening Now?

You may be surprised when your IFS couples therapist asks you, "What does it feel like inside when you say that?" or, "Is that part here now?" You might feel like he or she interrupted you, or that it is strange to look for the actual presence of a part.

IFS couples therapy, and IFS therapy in general, focuses

on your actual, felt experience in the moment. In fact, effective therapy always includes actual, moment-to-moment experiences (Lewis, Amini & Lannon, 2000). It might seem strange at first, but if you take a leap of faith and look for the actual presence of a part, you will get much more out of therapy. Focusing on how you feel in the moment as you discuss problems with your partner will allow you to express more of yourself, and it will help you and your partner have more productive, connected discussions.

Getting to Exiles

IFS couples therapists know that extreme behavior (anger, lying, controlling, distancing) is the work of Managers and Firefighters protecting Exiles. Therefore, couples therapy often focuses on finding and getting to know Exiles. When and if you are ready, your couples therapist will invite you to get to know the hurt parts within you and help them feel less isolated and afraid.

Focusing on You or Your Partner Individually

Sometimes your IFS couples therapist will talk to you and your partner as a couple and sometimes to one of you individually.

When your couples therapist focuses on you as a couple, you will get a chance to communicate directly with your partner about the issues that are most important to you. As Harville Hendrix, the founder of Imago Relationship Therapy (1988), says, "Couples therapy is most productive when partners take turns listening to each other with curiosity, empathy, and attention." Your IFS couples therapist will divert you from mutual dialogue if there are parts in the way of proceeding productively. When your couples therapist speaks to you directly, you will have a chance to get to know what blocks better communication with your partner. If all you need to do is acknowledge your Managers and Firefighters and have them step aside, this could take a few minutes. If you need to get to an Exile, it could take several hours over several sessions. Perhaps you and your partner will want to stay together in the room during this process. If your partner remains, he or she will be touched by the pain that is driving your anger, criticism, or distance, and by your openness, courage, and vulnerability. He or she might be able to contribute reactions or comments that enrich the process.

Perhaps you would rather do this individual work privately. You might feel safer talking to the couples therapist alone. When your partner returns, you can share what you discovered.

Either way, once you have focused on your parts, you will be back to interacting with your partner with renewed creativity and confidence.

What About My Individual Therapy?

Perhaps you or your partner is in individual therapy. You may be wondering how that will blend with couples therapy.

Once you start couples therapy, you may experience challenges and transitions in your individual therapy. Previously, you may have felt validated and appreciative when your individual therapist made judgments about your partner or gave you relationship advice. Once in couples therapy, you may wonder what to trust— your individual therapist who knows you so well, or the process that's unfolding in couples therapy.

Perhaps your individual therapist has tried to help by offering opinions about your relationship. Maybe he or she was concerned about your well-being and wanted you to consider leaving the relationship, or has offered opinions about your partner as a way to help you clarify your own experience. Perhaps you were tempted to use your individual therapy to complain about your partner and your therapist allowed you to do this.

Once you start couples therapy, it could be difficult for you if your individual therapist keeps offering advice and opinions. You might need to go through a transition with your individual therapist and find out what things to reserve for the couples therapy.

It is possible that you act differently in your individual therapy than you do in your couples therapy. The presence of your partner may bring out parts of you that you don't show to your individual therapist. As a result, it may be hard for your individual therapist to understand what is happening in your couples therapy and for the couples therapist to understand what is happening in your individual therapy.

If any conflicts arise, you can discuss them with both your individual and couples therapists. Hopefully, you can resolve them so that your couples therapy has the best chance to succeed, and you can continue enjoying the benefits of your individual therapy.

CHAPTER 14

For IFS Therapists

Are you an IFS trained therapist wondering how to use IFS in couples therapy? Have you heard of IFS, and wonder how it works in couples therapy? Or are you already using IFS in couples therapy and want some ideas? This chapter is for you.

This chapter highlights how IFS couples therapy is different from other approaches, how it can be helpful, and how you might use it in various situations..

The Goal of IFS Couples Therapy

The goal of IFS couples therapy is to release Self energy in one or both partners so that they can access Self qualities (creativity, confidence, connection, calm, clarity, curiosity, compassion, and courage). Once they have access to these innate characteristics, they will have the resources they need to solve their relationship problems.

Perhaps you are wondering:

Why is the goal to release the Self energy of one or both partners? Shouldn't it always be both?

Why are Self qualities innate?

How can we be sure that partners have the resources they need? Don't some people have deficits and need education or help to develop new capacities? Don't people have attachment problems and need a therapeutic relationship to heal?

Isn't the couples therapist supposed to solve the couple's problems?

Isn't couples therapy supposed to be about the relationship, not the two individuals?

These questions highlight the uniqueness of IFS couples therapy. Let's start with the first question: Why is the goal of IFS couples therapy to release Self energy in one or both partners?

IFS Couples Therapy Helps One or Both Partners Release Self Energy

Each partner in a couple has the capacity to release or stay in Self energy regardless of what the other person is doing. While IFS couples therapy is about both people, and both are probably contributing to the problem, the IFS couples therapist believes that one person's change is not contingent on the other's. One person can change their reactions regardless of what the other one is doing. Usually one person's change triggers the other person to change. Even if it doesn't, the one who has changed has accessed Self energy, and will be able to participate in the relationship and deal with challenges more effectively.

Each partner is 100% responsible for their contribution to the problem. When a partner takes care of their 100%, then they know they aren't contributing to the problem. They can also calmly observe the effects of their actions. Then they will have clarity to assess whether the relationship is viable. Perhaps they will see better behavior from their partner and feel a renewed bond. Or perhaps they won't see enough change and will face a difficult choice. Either way, they have more clarity and calm within themselves.

Self is the Best Relationship Problem-Solver

Self qualities are always available, even under painful relationship conditions, and when released, they uncover creative, connected, and clear problem solving and communication.

When partners communicate with Self energy, they automatically use good problem-solving skills. You'll find that you don't have to teach these skills—they emerge on their own when Self energy is present. Since Self energy is so effective, it's a better use of your efforts to focus on removing the barriers to Self energy than on teaching problem-solving skills.

When one person has access to Self energy, they automatically stop shaming and blaming. Self doesn't need to demean another person. Self energy does not attack, so the other partner's Firefighters have nothing to fight against. They may keep reacting for a while out of habit, but when they see there is still no attack, shame, or judgment, they won't have the fuel to continue.

Confidence is one of the innate Self qualities. When it arises, it illuminates connection, solutions, and courage. It makes life's situations workable and allows people to face their circumstances with optimism and intelligence. Partners with confidence can speak their truth without needing to push; stay true when they don't get the response they want; and say to themselves, "I did my best. Now I can see what kind of response I get."

Self energy helps partners assess each other. Partners sometimes come into couples therapy wondering if they should stay in the relationship. They vacillate between victimhood, anger, and hopelessness. No one can clearly and wisely assess their partner when buffeted by such strong, consuming emotions.

For example, imagine that one partner is angrily expressing her dissatisfaction. She cries about how unworthy she feels when she doesn't feel understood, panicking that her partner will leave her if she expresses her emotions. Finally, she collapses into hopelessness. Will this woman be able to see how her partner is responding? She will be so consumed by her emotions that she won't see her partner's face, hear his words and tone, or notice his body language. She won't have the data necessary to know if her partner's response is acceptable to her.

When partners are aware of how the other is responding, they have real data. They don't have to wonder if the other can listen, change, be kind, or be responsible. They can see it with their own eyes. Then they can make decisions based on reality.

If partners are in Self energy, they are better able to respond to positive input. The Self qualities of calm and creativity allow partners to respond to caring, thoughtful responses. If one partner softens, the other can build on that and create positive momentum. When partners are in Firefighter mode, bids for connection are perceived as threats, and the automatic response is defense or attack. It's hard to gain momentum when every vulnerable, kind, understanding response is met with suspicion and criticism. IFS couples therapists don't need to coach people to recognize and respond to positive bids—it happens naturally when there is Self energy.

Self energy helps partners find vital and nourishing commitment. When protectors are thinking about commitment, they might sound like this:

I choose you if you listen to me.
I choose you if you choose me.
I choose you if you change.

When Self energy is leading, thinking changes to:

I choose you knowing how difficult it can be for me when you don't listen. I want to remain present and connected when you do that. I choose that challenge.

I choose you because I want to. Sometimes it seems like I'm pursuing you, and that brings up reactions I need to explore.

It's hard to live with you when you are so (angry, addicted, cold, busy, sloppy, obsessively neat). I need to look at the parts in me that get triggered when you act that way. If I find I don't want this challenge anymore, I can work with the parts of me that are afraid to leave and find my courage and confidence.

IFS couples therapy helps partners accept the challenge the other partner brings, not change the partner to remove the challege. IFS therapists communicate, "If you choose this person, it means loving them and accepting them as they are; expressing your complaints with courage, connection, and curiosity; and working with the parts of you that might be afraid to say how upset you are or that think you don't deserve better treatment."

When it becomes clear that separation has to occur, Self energy helps partners do it with equanimity. It's more peaceful for partners to leave knowing that they did their best. When partners know they have communicated with Self energy, they won't have to wonder if they were the problem, or what would have happened if they had been able to be clear, courageous, and connected. They are freed from obsessive thoughts of self-doubt and blame. They can be peaceful, thoughtful, and resourceful, and move on without regret or self-criticism.

Separating couples often demonize each other. They may even enlist future partners in this, building and maintaining negative beliefs about the previous partner. This behavior burdens separated individuals, their children, and their future partners. It's much better to leave a relationship confident in your own contribution, free from the need to blame.

IFS Couples Therapy May Look Uneven at Times

Since the goal of IFS couples therapy is to access Self energy in one or both partners, it might look uneven at times. There may be more focus on one partner in a given session, or even over several sessions.

For example, if one partner works hard at getting to know the aspects of Self energy, it's not necessary to have the other partner immediately do the same.

Once when I was training therapists, I did a demonstration where I spent twenty-five minutes helping one partner give better back than they were receiving. Even though it was a role play couple, everyone in the room could feel that something significant shifted between the partners. After one partner gave better back, I helped her prepare for less than ideal responses she might receive so she could maintain her Self energy. Together, they talked about what might happen. "I could test you on the way home," the receiving partner said, "to see if you really mean it." I helped the giving-better-back partner prepare for that so she could stay in Self energy.

Some of the trainees asked, "Aren't you going to help the other partner give better back now? Aren't you going to make it fair?" I explained that instead of switching to the other partner, it was better to help the partner I already worked with prepare for bad reactions. At home, partners give better back, admit, and do all sorts of other good things—and the other partner isn't ready to reciprocate. They may say something nice and then revert to accusation and attack. It's best to be prepared for that, and be ready to stay centered no matter how the other responds. It's better for partners to stay calm and connected when they don't get what they want than to revert to non-Self-led behavior like blaming, distancing, and anger. In one session, there is rarely enough time to do this with both partners.

Self Qualities Are Innate

Since Self qualities are innate, IFS couples therapy focuses on:

Releasing love, not building it
Releasing problem-solving abilities, not teaching them
Releasing healthy attachment, not developing it
Releasing Self energy between the partners, not creating it

Releasing is different from building, teaching, developing, or creating.

The IFS model proposes that everyone, no matter how damaged, has pristine, whole Self energy available to them. They can be loving, skillful, securely attached, and Self-led without being coached or taught. The action of IFS couples therapy is more about removing obstacles than building skills.

Many models of couples therapy suggest that the therapist train couples to communicate well, teaching "I" messages, expressing feelings, taking turns, and avoiding judgmental speech. IFS couples therapy favors removing obstacles so couples can do these things automatically.

The primary role of an IFS couples therapist is to help partners remove the obstacles to problem solving. Therefore, the IFS couples therapist de-emphasizes coaching, advice, and modeling. For example, (I hope) I've never recommended a "date night" or that people who complain about not having sex should just go home and do it. People have already thought of these obvious solutions. There are deeper reasons for the problems couples experience. Their own internal systems are coming up with ideas, counteracting them with other plans, and then judging and criticizing for the lack of solutions.

It's more efficient to look at what's in the way than to take sides with any of these internal positions. I'd rather ask, "How does it work well not to have sex?" than to tell someone they should have more of it.

Suggestions from the couples therapist may indeed work, but the benefits are usually temporary. Long-lasting, robust solutions come from Self energy.

Isn't Couples Therapy Supposed to Be about the Relationship, Not the Two Individuals?

Even though IFS couples therapy often focuses on releasing Self energy in one partner at a time, it is not just individual therapy with the other person present. The difference is that the therapist focuses on the parts that get in the way of couple communication. Partners might present with parts that need help, but the IFS couples therapist doesn't focus on them unless they are blocking the couple's communication.

There are many ways to identify these relationship-blocking parts. Often you can find them when the partners talk to each other about their issues, and you watch for anything other than Self qualities. Another good method is sculpture, where one partner moves the other into the position that demonstrates how they are at their worst. Then you can see what exactly is triggering the sculptor, and you can ask about parts that are upset.

Here are the steps you can use to do sculpture with couples:

1. Decide on a particular problem the couple wants to improve.

2. Get clear on what each one does to trigger the other.

3. Decide which partner will be the sculptor.

4. Get permission from the sculptee to let the sculptor give him or her words to say, a tone with which to say them, and to gently move them into a particular position.

5. Ask the sculptor what the other partner should do or say to trigger them into their difficult experience.

6. Have the sculptee practice a few times to get it right.

7. When the sculptor is ready, have the sculptee say/do the behavior.

8. The sculptor moves the sculptee's arms, legs and body into the position that best expresses how they perceive the sculptee as they say/do the behavior.

9. At this point, the focus goes to the parts of the sculptor. You can ask them to sculpt themselves into the position that best expresses how they feel when they receive the words and behavior from the sculptee. Here is where you will find your target part and move into parts-Self relationship.

Shifting to the IFS Lens: Gains and Losses

Shifting your focus from other models of couples therapy to IFS can bring vitality, freshness, and surprising effectiveness to your couples therapy practice. But it also involves losses. The IFS approach leaves less time to use the good methods you learned from other models. In fact, sometimes using interventions from other models postpones or diminishes the effectiveness of IFS couples therapy.

Psycho-education is not prominent in IFS couples therapy. You probably know a lot of helpful research and experience-based information. As you do more IFS couples therapy, you may find yourself holding back on offering this information in lieu of helping the couple find their own solutions. IFS is often about therapists not knowing the solution, which leaves room for Self to know.

In IFS terms, psycho-education can be ineffective because protectors do not want to be educated. They want to do their jobs. As long as they feel their jobs are necessary, protectors can interpret psycho-education as an attempt to fight or bypass them. Since they are protecting out of love and necessity, they will resist.

Here are some things to try if you want to shift to the IFS approach.

Instead of making suggestions, educating, or coaching,
Try appreciating the protectors for what they do.

Example: A woman has a hard time accepting a compliment from her partner. You could probably think of many creative ways to help her with this. You may ask her to try an experiment and let in a little positive feedback. This is wonderful, but it's not IFS. The IFS approach might sound something like this: "What part of you doesn't want to accept compliments? Is it here now? Would it be willing to tell you the good reasons why it doesn't want you to accept compliments?"

Instead of suggesting, "Why don't you just try to have more sex, listen better, or go on a date night,"
> **Try finding out what's in the way of doing these things.**

Instead of managing reactivity (bells, coaching, educating),
> **Try asking parts why they have to be so intense/dedicated/sure.**

Instead of teaching careful language,
> **Try asking parts why they don't want to listen, express curiosity, or be respectful.**

Instead of you figuring out if the couple's relationship is healthy for them,
> **Try to get obstacles out of the way so courage and clarity can emerge from the partners themselves.**

Ask tough questions and have the partners come to their own conclusions. Self energy includes courage, confidence, and clarity, so it doesn't necessarily mean accepting a situation.

Instead of talking about, explaining, or analyzing behavior,
> **Try facilitating direct in-the-moment relationships between Self and parts, encouraging them to explain their actions themselves.**

Instead of figuring out who the problem is,
> **Try helping each partner stay in Self energy, regardless of the other's behavior, helping them meet the challenges of the other person.**

Instead of fighting protectors,
> **Try understanding and validating the important work protectors do (see the heart flip below).**

Instead of acknowledging and understanding the pain driving defensive or immature behavior yourself,

Try helping Self hear it directly from Exiles and protectors.

Instead of figuring out why defensive behavior is present yourself,

Try helping Self hear it directly from protectors.

Instead of assessing developmental deficits,

Try finding out why parts had to take extreme roles which look like developmental deficits.

Beginning IFS Couples Therapy Sessions

There are many ways to begin the first sessions of IFS couples therapy. Below are a few approaches that may work well for you.

I tell people that the first session will be fifty to sixty minutes long. It will be a time to see if we make a good team, if I can help, and for them to evaluate me. "We'll decide how to proceed," I say, "either at the end of the first or second session or after you have a chance to talk about it privately."

I rarely, if ever, start focusing on parts in the first session. I find it more important to connect with the partners and see how my parts are reacting. I don't think there is enough trust in the first session to plunge into unblending or into parts-Self relationships. You will see some questions below that refer to parts by name or in spirit, but you don't have to go any further than that.

In the first session, I want to find out what the problems are and if I can help. I like to make a list of each partner's complaints, verbatim if possible. Eventually, these will become fuel for parts exploration. As you will see in Step One below, it's okay to conclude that you can't help someone. In fact, it's more than okay; it's actually unethical to treat someone that you know you can't help.

Here are questions you may find useful in the first session:

Are you coming for enrichment or crisis?

Does one of you want to be here more than the other?

How much time are you spending together? What is it like?

How is sex/intimacy going? (This question lets everyone know that sex is an acceptable topic, and the sooner you mention it, the sooner people know it's okay to discuss. If you delay, it may be harder to bring it up later.)

If there are red flags or special circumstances, ask pointed questions. For example:

> In the case of an affair: Is the affair over? Do you both agree that it's over? Why don't you think it's over?
>
> Why is it urgent to make this relationship work? What are your concerns if it doesn't?
>
> Do you need this therapy to save the marriage? Why? Could you accept the ending of the relationship if it happened?
>
> If the only acceptable result is saving the marriage, I may not be the right person for you. I need you to know that the only way I can do my best work is to be neutral about the outcome. I know you say you are willing to do anything you can to restore your partner's love, but it is possible that your efforts won't succeed.
>
> Why is it so crucial that your partner change? Would it work for you if he/she stayed the same but you didn't have to react the way you do?

If one partner has no complaints:

> Do you have any complaints? Do you think this couples therapy is only about your partner's complaints?

You may want to consider not taking a formal history in the first session. Except for finding out about danger to self or others, violence, mental illness, medication, or other crucial information, you may want to wait to hear their history within the context of personal meaning. They may tell you they have had couples therapy before, or that they were abandoned as a child, but until you know how their parts made meaning out of it, it won't be as useful to you. Their meaning is unique to them, and it may not coincide with what you already know.

Ten Steps to IFS Couples Therapy

These ten steps will guide you in IFS couples therapy. They may not progress in precise order, and some may not be as important as others for particular couples, but each addresses an important aspect of the IFS couples therapy process.

Step One: Make Sure the Conditions for Couples Therapy Are Present

Are the foundations and conditions for successful couples therapy present? Do your own assessment. Possibly also engage the partners in their assessment of their readiness for couples therapy. If you have any concerns about the conditions, be sure to discuss them with the couple as soon as possible.

You may approach the first session wanting the couple to feel connected, safe, and at ease with you. Those are worthy objectives, but don't let that obscure your clarity about the conditions for couples therapy. If the conditions aren't right, therapy probably won't go well. As a result, the couple may lose hope in therapy in general. Assessing the conditions and sometimes saying no to a couple is protecting and serving them, not denying help.

As you do more couples therapy, you may gain clarity about the conditions you need in order to do your best work. Here are three questions to pay particular attention to:

1. Can you do what the couple wants you to do?
2. Are you the right therapist for this couple?
3. Does the couple have the resources they need to do couples therapy the way you want to do it?

Can You Do What the Couple Wants You to Do?

Most of the time couples want help and you can give it. But sometimes you will need to get extra clarity about what the couple wants you to do for them. If they aren't clear, find out why, and inquire about whether the partners have different goals. It's better to get as much understanding as you can in the beginning, before you have made a commitment to treat them. Sometimes you may need to actively confront partners about their goals.

Once you know what the couple wants, ask yourself if you can do it. If you skip this step, therapy may stagnate, or partners may become disappointed or angry with you.

Here is a list of therapy goals that may not work.

Make Him/Her Change

Partners usually criticize each other and want each other to change. Given the opportunity to look at it differently, most will shift to more fruitful goals. However, in the rare cases when one or both partners are unwavering in their insistence that the other changes, couples therapy may not be viable. If you hear things like, "He/she needs to stop raging/drinking/gambling/being sloppy/working too much," follow up with questions. It may be true that such changes would be beneficial, but couples therapy is not about one person changing. You could ask, "Is that your only goal? Is there anything you are contributing to the problem? Is there anything you want to change in yourself?" The complaining partner will usually talk about his or her own participation in the problem or express willingness to look at it. Then you will have established a firm footing for couples therapy involving both partners. If you skip this step, partners may think you are agreeing that the goal of the therapy is to change one person rather than to help both. Successful couples therapy has to involve both partners. If both partners really agree that one person has to change, individual therapy is probably better.

Join Me in Condemning Him/Her

It is not a problem if partners begin couples therapy with blame, shame, and condemnation. The IFS therapist knows these attitudes come from protector parts, and that gentle understanding of the good the part is trying to do is often enough to create a shift. But what if that doesn't work?

If one partner can't stop blaming and shaming, you might ask the other partner to wait outside for thirty minutes while you talk to the one casting blame. Sometimes it's easier for people to focus on their own blaming parts without the other partner present. That's often enough to find and validate a protector, and to enable the person to speak for it, but not from it.

What if you make multiple attempts to welcome and understand judgmental parts and a partner is still unable to shift away from blaming and shaming? Or what if the partner briefly stops judging and then reverts? That could mean it's not the right time for the partner to give up their judgment and participate in productive couples therapy. It is often better to name this and suggest that they come back when they can work differently with their judging parts, or that individual therapy might be a good idea before couples therapy.

Help Us Fix Our Relationship While Our Divorce Lawyers Litigate

When divorce lawyers are actively litigating, it is not in partners' best interest to open up in couples therapy. Anything they say could be used against them in court. You could receive a court order for the records or be instructed to appear personally. These are not conditions under which people can or should be vulnerable. What if they are open with each other and then hear from their lawyer that they should use that vulnerability in litigation? I tell partners that I will work with them if they put their litigation completely on hold. They have to tell their lawyers and their lawyers need to agree. All court processes need to stop, with no pending responses or activities. Many couples are willing to do this.

Help Us Fix This Marriage While an Affair Continues

Couples therapy is usually a bad idea during an active affair. It's unsafe and unfair for the faithful partner to open up and be vulnerable while the unfaithful partner is still seeing someone, still in love with someone, or has just put the affair "on hold" for the duration of the couples therapy.

Affairs are active if there is still emotional contact via phone, email, text, or in person. It may be unclear to you—and the partners—whether contact is over. Sometimes the affair partner says it's over and the faithful partner has doubts. You can use those doubts to query the affair partner and clarify the situation. If you have suspicions and the faithful partner doesn't, you can explore why.

Affairs are still active if the affair partner is still in love. Regardless of whether they are seeing or communicating with the other person, being in love with the other person means the affair is continuing. If the affair partner wants to fall out of love with the other person and fall back in love with their mate, couples therapy may be viable. If the unfaithful partner really wants to be with the other person, he or she might be putting off the inevitable, perhaps out of fear of hurting their mate, from a lack of courage, or for practical reasons. In this case, it is not fair to ask the faithful partner to be vulnerable in front of the unfaithful one.

You can be very direct in your questioning as long as you aren't judgmental. As always, do the heart flip (see below) before you speak. If you are judgmental about the affair or about the faithful partner, you won't be effective and parts won't trust you.

I/We Want a Specific Outcome

Sometimes one or both partners want couples therapy to provide a specific outcome. Often, after you connect and offer other opportunities, they realize they can be open to more options. However, if they are very clear and persistent about wanting a specific outcome, couples therapy may not be viable. You can't do your best work and welcome all parts if you are constrained by a particular goal. Self energy doesn't work that way either.

The most common request is for you to make the relationship work, or make one partner love the other again. Partners may come to you desperate for their relationship to work and look to you for tools to fix it. It's important to explain that you can't guarantee the outcome and that couples therapy could lead to ending the relationship. Make it clear that you are neutral about whether the relationship continues or ends. If you don't, one or both partners could get very angry with you. Also, if you are not neutral, you may not be able to be present to all the parts in the room.

Similarly, if one partner thinks couples therapy is about helping the other one fall in love again, it's important to tell them that you can't commit to that specific outcome. If one partner is truly done, couples therapy could help him or her get clear, courageous, and ready to leave.

Sometimes one partner is motivated to change, work on their issues, and do anything that will get the other person to love them again. It may be very tempting for you to jump in and help that partner with his/her parts, but if they think there is a guarantee that their personal work will lead to reconciliation, they may feel disappointed, angry, or betrayed if it doesn't. Beware of helping desperate people change their behavior to get an outcome. It can often be more effective to work with the partner who has fallen out of love. You may find parts that, when given attention, allow love to come back, or parts blocking the courage to leave.

It's good general psychotherapy practice to avoid agreeing to a specific outcome. If people have a certain goal, and you say or imply that psychotherapy can make it happen, it's not fair to them and it constricts you. It's also not good legal practice. Some people will make malpractice, ethics, or licensing complaints when they feel misled.

You might see this as a contract. "Contract" might sound cold and legalistic, but in fact, your professional organization probably requires you to begin therapy with an informed consent contract, and to continue to educate clients about the contract as new situations arise. Clients have access to legal means (malpractice, ethics, and licensing complaints) if they think you agreed to do one thing and did another, or if it caused experiences or events for which they weren't prepared.

The partners may not agree on the desired outcome. If one partner accepts that separation may be an outcome, the other may say that is not acceptable. You may need to get clarity from both partners and an agreement that they can tolerate different outcomes.

We Want Couples Therapy but We Are Not Prepared for the Risks
It's important to make sure both partners are prepared for the risks of couples therapy. You may be accustomed to telling your individual clients that they may experience intense sadness, guilt, anger, frustration, loneliness, and helplessness during the course of therapy. Couples risk having those feelings and also the possibility of separation, divorce, financial and child-rearing losses, loss of social networks, and intense heartbreak. Be respectful of them and yourself and tell couples that couples therapy may bring pain and loss. If there is any doubt that they are able and willing to tolerate such sad and challenging experiences, explore it and decide whether you can continue.

One particular concern is financial stress. Some partners believe that they cannot separate. For instance, a young mother with small children and no substantial income might feel that she cannot leave her husband. Couples therapy may not work in some of these cases because fear will limit the conversations and the outcomes.

We Want Parenting Education

Sometimes couples who are ending or have ended their relationship seek couples therapy for help with co-parenting. Perhaps they separated while they were in couples therapy with you, or perhaps they are calling you for the first time for this specific purpose. If you agree to this, be aware that there are differences between parenting education and couples therapy. Couples therapy requires both partners to be vulnerable, sometimes in ways that are new and scary, for the goal of increased intimacy. The goal of parenting education is to coordinate and cooperate in parenting for the good of the children, not necessarily to increase intimacy between the parents.

Once a relationship has ended, it can be confusing and counterproductive for partners to keep trying to grow together in intimacy. Once partners have decided to separate, their relationship must change. They have done all they can do to grow together as partners. They may grow in their understanding of what happened over the years and learn more about themselves and their contribution. They may grow in friendship, but the growth of partnered intimacy is over.

Upon separation, it might be more productive for the individuals to mourn together, and shift to the goals of friendliness, goodwill, collaboration, and respect.

Be clear about what you believe is good for separated couples and what you can offer. I have found that I cannot shift away from helping couples deepen intimacy, so I do not do parenting education. When separating couples want to see me a bit longer, I try to make it clear that we'll be very limited in what we can do. Often one partner is not ready to separate and needs a few sessions to feel held and comforted while they adjust.

I Want You to Keep a Secret

What are you going to do if partners tell you secrets in a phone call, through email, at the beginning of a session (if you let one enter before the other arrives), or in individual sessions? It's best to make your policy clear before there is the possibility of private communication.

According to the American Psychological Association Trust legal counsel, there is only one ethical option. You may not keep secrets or withhold anything from either partner. You are treating both partners, and you are not serving them well if you keep secrets.

This issue may come up if you do any individual sessions with the partners in the service of the couples therapy. That is ethical to do, but if one partner reveals in an individual session that he or she is done with the relationship, you cannot keep this a secret. You also can't keep meeting with that partner individually. Once a partner has made it clear they want to separate, and the other one doesn't agree, you can't support the separating partner in individual sessions. They may need help becoming more clear and courageous, but you cannot be the one to provide it. Your duty and commitment is to both partners, and you can't offer individual help to one partner if the outcome would hurt the other. Of course, all of this can be freely discussed in joint sessions with the partners.

We Want Couples Therapy, but We Don't Have the Resources
Couples therapy takes time and money. If partners don't have the needed resources, couples therapy may fail, and the couple may lose faith in therapy in general. It's best to assess whether couples have the time and money for couples therapy.

Perhaps a couple wants therapy but can't come regularly because of scheduling or financial limitations. Couples therapy needs momentum in the beginning; usually that means weekly sessions (barring illness or vacation). If they don't come regularly, you may find yourself starting over each time you meet. Instead of moving forward, you may spend most of your time dealing with protectors who have emerged between sessions and interrupted the progress.

Sometimes you may want to do individual sessions to augment the couples therapy. Do they have the time to add those sessions in, and do you have the time? Can they come when you are available?

Perhaps a couple can come regularly, but they can't pay for

the length or number of sessions necessary. I need seventy-five to ninety minutes per session to do effective IFS couples therapy. It takes me time to connect, find something to focus on, focus at the right level, come out of it, involve the other partner if they have been silent, and then prepare for the week to come. How much time do you need?

If couples don't have the time or resources for what they need, it might be better to postpone the therapy until they do. Otherwise the therapy may not work and the couple will lose hope in therapy.

I Want Couples Therapy, but I Am Letting My Individual Therapist Judge My Partner

Individual therapists can have a big impact on couples therapy. They may support their client's efforts to explore their contribution to the problem. They can also tell you useful things about how the client processes the couples therapy. Unfortunately, they may join with their client in judging, diagnosing, or criticizing the other partner.

I ask clients if they use their individual therapy to criticize their partner. If they say yes, I explain this behavior will disrupt couples therapy. I ask if they are willing to tell their therapist they want to stop doing that so they can focus on their own issues. Sometimes this shift can easily happen and individual therapists are glad to get back to individual issues.

Get permission to speak to the individual therapist after a couple of sessions. It's best if you can get approval from both partners; otherwise you can't talk about the other partner at all. Unless I know the therapist very well, I usually stick to complimenting the client, asking if I could be a "fly on the wall" hearing how the person talks about their relationship in the individual therapy, and asking for any input that the individual therapist considers helpful. I have received useful information from these conversations.

Unless specifically asked, I generally stay away from telling the individual therapist negative things about the person's behavior in couples therapy. Individual therapists and couples therapists see different sides of the client. In individual therapy, the client and the therapist often have a warm, connected, positive relationship. They usually treat each other well. In couples therapy, the client may behave in ways the individual therapist never sees. For example, clients may talk about feeling hurt and victimized in individual therapy and then act more like a victimizer in couples therapy. They may tell their individual therapist that they don't feel heard or understood in their marriage, and in couples therapy, they may be the one who doesn't listen. The individual therapist may not see or hear about that behavior. It can be very confusing and disconcerting for an individual therapist to hear that their client is angry, defensive, distant, or bullying in couples therapy.

The phone call with the individual therapist is an opportunity to connect with the therapist, create a positive collaborative relationship, and avoid future splitting and polarization. Look for information that will help you as the couples therapist, and don't count on providing useful information to the individual therapist.

If your mutual client communicates to you or the individual therapist in ways that create polarization, your relationship with the individual therapist could become problematic.

If you feel judgmental toward an individual therapist, or if the individual therapist is upset with you, consider that your client may have said things to polarize you. Perhaps a client's parts, in their effort to protect the client, have created discord between you and the individual therapist.

It's best to try to get back to mutual positive regard with the individual therapist. You may not agree with each other about the dynamics or the solution, but having respect and understanding between the two of you can be enough. Then you can use the particulars of events to understand the client's protective system.

Am I the Right Therapist for This Couple?

A couple might be ready for couples therapy, but you may not be the right therapist for them. Here are a few situations you may encounter.

Conflicts with Your Personal Values

If you aren't supportive and relaxed about a couple's values, morals, or lifestyle, you may not be able to be a good couples therapist for them. May be you aren't overtly judgmental, but you might be cool or uncomfortable with some lifestyle choices. Be honest with yourself and bow out if you can't feel open-hearted about the way one or both partners live.

You Don't Like the Couple

If you don't like the couple, and you can't shift out of that in the first or second session, think seriously about whether you are the right therapist for them. In many cases, you can use your feelings of dislike to connect with Protectors and the Exiles they protect. Your initial lack of affection for them might be a part you can address quickly. If not, the whole therapy might be tepid and unproductive, and it might be best to withdraw. It's okay to admit to yourself that you don't like a couple. It's your parts, but you don't always have the ability to connect with all your parts.

Your Parts in Step One

You'll be working continually with your own parts all the way through the ten steps of IFS couples therapy. In this first step, watch out for parts of you that don't want to explore or admit that the conditions for couples therapy are absent. Also, make sure that you are the right person for them or that they have the necessary resources. For instance, you may think:

"I don't feel comfortable with these people, but I can't admit that. I should be comfortable and accepting of everyone."

Your discomfort may be your body's way of telling you that something is going on with the couple beneath the surface. One or both of the partners may be holding back information. Perhaps one partner is having an affair, wants out of the relationship, has an addiction, or is doing something illegal. Work with the parts of you that think you can't listen to your discomfort. When they calm down, you'll be able to ask questions and find out what's going on.

Another thought may be: "I have to help them. I'm supposed

to help anyone who comes to me. I have no choice."

You do have a choice about whether to treat a couple or not. In fact, you are ethically bound to make an informed choice. It's your responsibility to protect clients from therapy that, in your opinion, won't be productive.

For instance, are their lives so chaotic that they can't keep appointments? Do they keep getting into emergencies that prevent them from doing inner work? Are they so terrified of splitting up that they can't look at difficult issues? If you have any parts that think you have to help, work with them.

Here are some other things you may hear yourself thinking:

"This will be a heroic effort. I'll be extending myself beyond what I can do, but I can push myself to do it."

Again, this may be useful information. You might be getting visions of heroism because the couple's living situation may not support couples therapy, it's not the right time for couples therapy, or there are secrets.

Another consideration: "I don't know how to help these people. But I can't admit that, because that would make me incompetent."

This is really important! If you don't know how to help, there may be valid reasons. If you can calm down the parts that think you have to know, you'll be able to enter a curious, confident state in which direct, appropriate questions come easily to you, and the reason for your lack of confidence becomes clear. Perhaps you don't have the specific expertise needed to help this couple, or perhaps the couple isn't ready.

You may think: "These people seem so sincere in their approach to psychotherapy, but I just don't think therapy is going to help them."

You may be picking up on something. Pay attention to this feeling, tell your parts it's fine to have this thought, and you may receive valuable information. For example, perhaps one or both partners lack the courage to face a separation, even though they know the relationship is over. It might be better to know that courage is missing before you plunge into the work of therapy.

Otherwise they might just drop out because they get scared.

Lastly, another thought may be: "I feel nervous. They will likely need more than one session a week, or longer sessions, or individual sessions. I don't know how we will be able to do that."

Maybe you don't have the time for additional sessions or the energy for another trauma situation. Perhaps the couple doesn't have the time, energy, or money. If you or they don't have the resources to do the work the way it needs to be done, it might be better not to do it. It's better to tell them what you think they need, and if they can't do it now, they can make the necessary preparations for a successful therapy experience in the future.

Your little voices and feelings could contain valuable information. Couples come in with unique situations. You can't always use your previous experience to assess a situation, but you can use your thoughts, feelings, and sensations. Have the courage to listen and feel into yourself. Take care of parts that get in the way of creative thinking. Then you'll be able to meet each couple system as it is, uncover essential information, and avoid unproductive courses of therapy.

Step Two: Find the Parts Specifically Creating the Stuck Place in the Couple

Once you've determined that the conditions for couples therapy are present, it's time to look for parts that are creating the stuck place between the partners. The assumption of IFS couples therapy is that if parts aren't in the way, Self can solve any problem. Maybe the solution will not be the one expected or desired, but it will be spacious, vibrant, and full of possibility.

Effective IFS couples therapy depends on focusing on parts in the way of Self energy between the two partners. Since couples therapy is for the relationship, you need to know how the parts play out between the partners. If you skip this step, you run the risk of focusing on parts that are tangential to the couple's difficulty.

You may find lots of parts who could use attention and healing. But if you start working with parts before you know which specific ones relate to the couple's issues, you may prolong the therapy, or even create a situation in which it will never feel complete.

There are many ways to get to the specific parts. One way is to ask the partners to talk to each other about their most important issues, and get permission to interrupt. Then watch for parts that get in the way of resolution.

Another way to find the real and immediate issue between the partners is to ask, "What is the worst that happens between you?" and keep asking until it is really clear.

Sculpture can also be useful to identify triggers, protectors, and Exiles.

You can also look for the absence of Self qualities. Has a partner lost their calm demeanor? If either partner is agitated, there are parts in the way. With Self energy present, partners can have any feeling and be calm at the same time. It's the same with all the other Self qualities. For example, are they being clear but not connected? If connection is missing, they won't be able to communicate effectively with each other. Rationality alone won't help feelings fly from one heart to the other.

Are the partners curious about each other as they talk about their perceptions and complaints? If curiosity is lacking, communication won't have a musical, luminous, flowing quality. It won't move into new places—and new places are what couples want.

It might be useful to check for connection, calm, and curiosity first, and then look for confidence, courage, clarity, and compassion. As the couple's conversation progresses, the need or lack of confidence, courage, or clarity may become clear. You may find one partner lacking confidence or courage and holding back for fear of what will happen if he or she is more direct.

You may find that the conversation is connected, calm, courageous, and curious, but also flat and repetitive. That means creativity is missing. Something is in the way if the conversation doesn't naturally flow into new places.

Compassion is particularly important once you start focusing on one partner's Exiles. The other partner must be in a compassionate place or it will be a damaging experience for the partner who is opening up.

When you have found a specific part that is central to the couple's problem, start working on it as soon as you can. It's not necessary to allow the conversation to devolve into disconnection, recrimination, or distance. They do that at home, and they are looking for something different from you.

You will find parts in both people, but you can only work with one partner at a time. Trust your judgment. As long as your parts are not in the way, you will find and focus on the right part in the right partner.

Your Parts in Step Two

You may find that you are either too slow or too fast in finding the specific parts that are creating the stuck place in the couple. You personally may have parts that want to go fast and find a part as soon as possible. Perhaps these parts think you need to be useful and start doing good work quickly. These parts may want you to work with the first part that shows up before you know if it is the part that will free the couple's relationship.

Conversely, you may have personal parts that procrastinate, continually noticing and tracking parts, but not focusing on them. Maybe these parts want to use other models instead of IFS (educating, providing skills), or maybe they doubt your ability to unburden parts. You can reassure those parts that you will take it a step at a time and prove to them that the IFS process works.

Your slow or fast parts may also be picking up information in the couple's system. Maybe the fast parts sense that the partners are desperate and need help right away. Maybe the slow parts sense fragility. If you notice unusually slow or fast pacing, listen to your parts. They may have valuable information about the partners.

Since you are paying attention to parts that intersect between the partners, you may have reactions to how the partners treat each other. There are many dynamics that could be triggering.

For example, differences in sexual needs or needs for intimacy, abandonment, or soothing. Bullying is one of the most incendiary situations. Because it is so common and difficult to deal with, it's worth particular attention. How do you react to bullying? Does it trigger any of your parts? Do you react differently to men or women bullies?

Women may act differently than men when they are consumed by their bullying parts. They may alternate between bullying and victimhood. Male partners of women with bullying parts may find it difficult to admit they feel bullied for fear of appearing weak.

You may have reactions to men consumed by bullying parts. Maybe you are scared or intimidated. Maybe you judge the other partner for staying with such a person.

If there is a bullying dynamic and you aren't aware of it, or you are triggered by it, the whole couples therapy could fail. Pay attention to little voices you hear inside yourself. For instance:

> I don't like him/her
> She/he isn't a nice person
> I have to overlook her bullying behavior because she's a woman
> I'm afraid of him/her
> She/he should leave
> I have to protect the bullied person

These little voices could be clues that you have parts in the way of relating with bully parts. Once you take care of your parts, you'll be able to interact creatively with people acting like bullies or any other relationship dynamic that triggers you. You'll be able to keep your role as the couples therapist, wisely assess whether the bullying behavior is workable, and engage the couple in dealing with it.

Step Three: Get Clear on the Triggers

As you focus on specific parts, notice what triggers each partner's reaction. What happens just before a partner goes into a protector part? Or, more accurately, what does the triggered partner think the other partner did? That's the trigger.

For example, one partner might say she feels lonely, unmet, or misunderstood. What does she think her partner did to make her feel that way? What's the tone, phrase, or gesture that "causes" this loneliness?

You can observe triggers, you can ask about them, and you can use sculpture. When one partner reacts, ask them to explain or demonstrate what the other partner did to make them feel that way. The other partner is the "clay" or the "actor taking direction," and tries to get it right.

When you know what the triggers are, you'll be able to come back to them at the end of the session, and test the IFS principle that releasing Self energy in one partner can change the system.

After you have worked with the partner who was triggered and helped them get to know the parts that reacted to the trigger, you can ask the other partner to redo the same triggering behavior from the beginning of the session. You will see that the response won't be the same with Self energy.

Step Four: Do the Heart Flip

When you look for parts causing the couple's problem, you will probably find Firefighters. Are they very appealing? Not usually. That's not their job. They are there to protect, not to connect. You may find yourself disliking and judging these parts at first. If your initial reaction to a protector is cool or judgmental, don't say a word until you do the heart flip.

When you first meet a Firefighter, you may notice that your heart feels hard or contained, rather than soft, open, and warm. Can you flip your heart into openness? Maybe you can actually see an image of your heart flipping or changing. Perhaps you can feel the hard, tight sensations in your chest shift to tender openness. Or maybe your thoughts shift from, "He is so distant and arrogant," to "His protectors must think he really needs them. I wonder what happened to make them work so hard." Get to know what it's like for you to change from judgment to genuine interest.

Remember, the protectors you are judging exist out of love, loyalty, and concern. There may not have been a way to survive without strong protector activity. Once you have an open heart, you can begin a productive dialogue with protectors and enter into the world that made them take extreme roles.

It may be harder to do the heart flip in couples therapy than in individual therapy. Even though we know we cannot be effective unless we connect with both partners, we might find ourselves becoming unconsciously judgmental, dismissive, or fearful of one or the other. Below are six common reasons that the heart flip can be harder in couples therapy than in individual therapy.

1. One of the partners may be different than your usual type of client.

    Since opposites attract, you will probably be sitting with two very different people. If you are used to working with introspective people, you may find they are partnered with people who are more concrete. Are you used to helping people troubled by guilt? They may have partners who come across as remorseless. Are you skilled at helping people who experience themselves as victims? Get ready—they may have partners who come across as bullies. These opposites are great opportunities to flush out your own parts and get to know them.

2. You are in a triangle.

    What does that bring up in you? Do you feel like you have to help? Do you feel overwhelmed or helpless? Whatever it is, get to your own parts. You may find some of them stuck in old triangle experiences.

3.   Eroticism is in the room.

Even if a couple hasn't had sex for a long time, they probably have thoughts and feelings about it. Do you have any parts that are uncomfortable with this? Join the club! Get to know these parts and you'll be fine.

4.   Parts detecting in couples therapy is usually more complicated than it is in individual therapy.

When a new couple walks in the door, you will often encounter anomalous, unusual, triggering, confusing, and even scary situations. Not being able to easily predict or understand situations can be very triggering. Do you think you have to understand right away? Know how to help? Be intelligent? Your parts may think so. If they hurry, you may not have time to find the parts causing the block in the couple.

5.   Attachment issues are more intense and immediate.

Clients in individual therapy often have attachment issues with their significant others or with you. You may spend some time getting to know the client, talking "about" the relationship issues, and even experiencing a bit of the intensity in the therapy relationship. In couples therapy, the main attachment figure is right there in the room. Before you have even gotten to know your new clients, you could witness desperation, anxiety, stonewalling, and severe distress. You may see frightened or frightening behavior, intrusiveness, withdrawal, negativity, and wildly inaccurate affective responses. Maybe partners will alternate aggression and withdrawal with no seeming rational reason, or make and cancel bids for connection with breakneck speed.
     All of these situations are manageable. Just work with your parts that think they need to help, and you'll find the wisdom you need.

6. It is dangerous to sit back and just be present.

In individual therapy, you can sometimes be helpful by
listening and following silently. While there are times when it
is perfectly fine to wait, listen, and simply experience a couple
without intervening, there are more times when you will
need to be active. You may have to find your discriminating
wisdom much more quickly in couples therapy. Parts of you
that want to spend more time just experiencing the couple
may feel deprived. In individual therapy, you can often let
a session end on a note of distress and anxiety, anticipating
that the client will reflect on their experience before the
next session. Couples who end a session on a distressed note
can do a lot of damage between sessions. It's important to
think ahead and try to end couples therapy sessions on a
resolved note.

7. If you can't do the heart flip quickly.

The more couples you see, the more chance there is that you
will come to the end of a first session without being able to flip
your heart. That, of course, is a parts detector opportunity for
you. But it could also mean you may not be able to work with
the couple.

Sometimes Self energy means facing the possibility that
you aren't the best therapist for a particular couple. If you
can't get judging, distant, or fearful parts to step aside, it
might be better for you to refer them to a different therapist.

In order to leave room for this possibility, you can describe
the first few sessions as a time to meet and see how you function
as a team. You can invite clients to evaluate you. Tell them
that you will be evaluating if you can help them and if you are
the best therapist for them. If you leave this preamble out, it
may be more difficult to refer a couple to someone else.

Step Five: Can the Other Partner Be Present

Once you find a specific part and do the heart flip, you will need to find out if the other partner can be compassionate and present. You will soon be focusing on a part, possibly a vulnerable one. Can they be connected, interested, calm, and kind?

You can ask the other partner if they are okay if you talk to their partner for a while rather than to them. If they agree, does their answer seem genuine? Do they have a part that wants to be compliant or wishes they could be present? Are they unaware of parts that can't do that yet?

If they can't relax and be present, they may react when you focus on the other partner. When and if you get to an Exile, they may blurt out something like, "But what about me?" or "I feel incredibly threatened by all this" or "That's why I can't be with you." At the end, after their partner has connected with Exiles and unburdened, they may judge or attack. This could be very hurtful to the partner who just opened up.

Keep checking with the witnessing partner as the target partner goes deeper. What if you get to an Exile? Can the witnessing partner still be present? What if the target partner is going to reveal something sensitive—is the witnessing partner ready to hear the revelation?

It is okay to put off inner work until the other partner can be present because it is better not to do it than to do it and have it go badly.

This may be a very difficult step when both partners have been seriously traumatized. Partners may think they can be present and then surprise everyone when they are taken over by protectors. Sometimes you do your best to take care of the witnessing partner, and they still react hurtfully at the end of the session when you are out of time. Even when you plan ahead, it is still possible for traumatized partners to feel activated at the end of a session.

The best solution is to find and welcome parts that need to jump out at the end. You may find parts that have just one more thing they want to resolve and think they can do it in five minutes.

(They might benefit from a discussion about how much time it takes to do things.) Sometimes parts don't feel safe and don't want to leave until they can fix that.

Another approach is to leave lots of time at the end. Use half of your allotted time for couples work, and then start to wind down with the other half remaining. You may find that you accomplish significant work in the first half; and then, just as you begin to close, a huge new issue arises. You'll be glad you have time to deal with it.

You may also want to do some predicting at the beginning of the session. You might say something like: "I will do my best, and I hope we can work as a team to end this session on a peaceful note. However, that's not always possible. You may have parts jump out suddenly, without any idea that they were even listening. If we are out of time, we might have to end with an unresolved feeling. You can email or call me after the session, if that helps." This affirms that you understand how hard it is for them.

Step Six: Invitation to Unblend

Once you find a specific part, do the heart flip, and ensure that the other partner can be present, your next step is an invitation to unblend. Here is where you shift into true IFS mode. You've given up (for the moment) your other models, and you are going to follow IFS. You know that Self is available to help any part, but first, the part must unblend.

You will be asking your client to focus on something that may not feel like a part. It could feel weird to them to consider that an experience is a part and frightening to try something new.

You can grow your courage to introduce unblending in the face of fear and confusion. Remind your parts how well it's gone previously. Ask them to trust that the person really does want to focus on their own parts and that they will benefit.

Sometimes it takes multiple invitations before a part unblends. Just keep asking, using your creativity to find the right way.

Here are some questions you can ask to evoke interest in

unblending. They are just a few within the universe of your creativity.

> Would you like it if you could get your point across without criticism?

> Would you like it if he/she did that, and you didn't have to get so angry?

> Would you like it if you could complain connected?

> What if you could stay present, clear, calm, and grounded even if he/she keeps doing that?

If partners respond positively, you can explain that the next step is going to help them do that. You can ask:

> Would it be okay to notice how it feels inside when you say that?

> Would you like to try an experiment? I'll describe each step and you can decide if you want to continue. Then we'll consider the results.

Step Seven: Appreciate Why the Invitation to Unblend Is Refused

Unblending may happen the first time you ask, or it may not happen until the thirtieth. You may be able to proceed quickly, or you may find yourself on the zigzag path of protectors' objections.

You may deal with those concerns with a simple request to step aside, or you may switch your full attention to protectors. Whether it's direct or labyrinthine, your best approach is appreciation and open-heartedness toward protectors.

Sometimes you may need to stay with the objections for a whole session or even many sessions. It's far better to enter into the reality of the parts' recalcitrance, and offer acceptance and understanding, than to push them into something for which they are unprepared.

Step Eight: Find the Right Level of Focus

Once a part has unblended, you will need to find the right level of focus. The appropriate level is the one that loosens the knot between the couple.

Sometimes brief, heartfelt recognition of protectors will do it. This can release intimacy and spontaneous problem-solving. Maybe you have heard partners say something like, "I didn't realize that I was trying to punish him. Now that I see that, I don't want to do it anymore."

Perhaps you'll need a deeper level of focus, such as brief contact with an Exile. Protectors may step aside and allow enough access to create a shift.

Even deeper levels of focus include: establishing relationships with Exiles, witnessing their experiences, retrieving them from bad circumstances, and unburdening. You may need an entire session, or even multiple sessions, to focus on one person's Exiles, with the other partner sitting quietly most of the time. Sometimes it is more important to do this than to evenly divide your attention. If Exiles get the help they need, it will be good for both partners.

Some partners may need to see you individually to get to know their protectors and Exiles. You could work with them separately, but as part of the couples therapy, focusing only on issues that pertain to the couple. Explain that this is not individual therapy, but a supplement to couples therapy. Be sure to explain that professional ethics will not allow you to keep secrets revealed in individual sessions.

I find that this method works best when I request that the partners arrive together, but we make a plan to work with one person while the other waits in the waiting room. I find this approach supports the couples therapy better than having one partner arrive alone.

Step Nine: Bring It Back to Relationship

Once you've found the right level of focus and Self energy has been released, bring the couple back to the original problem. In the beginning, you noted what initially triggered a part, so you can say something like, "Remember when he asked you to move the salad plate and you got so upset? What would you do or say now if he did that?" Or you may ask, "Now would you like to go back to that incident you were talking about when she was being pushy? What would you do now?"

This is my favorite part of the process! I love the creativity that comes out when people bring Self energy to their problems. They say the funniest, most unexpected things—things I would never even imagine coaching them to say. Maybe you expect emotionally correct communication, structured in a careful, non-threatening way. It might not sound that way at all. But with Self energy present, it will be deep, light, spacious, humorous, connected, open-hearted, calm, and exciting. You'll love watching Self energy at work. I often say to myself, "I would never have thought of that. I'm so glad I didn't tell them what to do."

The other partner usually takes it very well. If they don't, the person with the Self energy can usually bear it without reacting. If not, you have a new target part.

Step Ten: Prepare for the Week Ahead

Whether you've had a great, game-changing session a difficult session, or an ordinary session, it is important to prepare the couple for the time between meetings.

If you have had a particularly moving session in which the partners have connected more deeply than normal, it is especially important to prepare them. Protectors may quickly jump back in and create disconnection. This is natural because protectors want to do their usual jobs. I usually tell couples that they should expect a break or disruption in the connection. If they prove me wrong, I'm happy; if not, they will be prepared for ups and downs. If you don't warn them, they may lose hope.

Just predicting a reversal is helpful. You can also give them some tools so they can deal with these experiences. Here are some statements I have found helpful:

It's like a rubber band snapping back to its usual shape—you may find yourself going right back to your old patterns before you know it.

Try to get the snapback over with as soon as possible. Since it's probably going to happen, you might as well have it happen as soon as possible and get back to connection.

When it happens, try to be light-hearted about it. Try to avoid going all the way into mutual disconnection. If you are the recipient of something negative (and we all feel like the recipient), try not to make it worse than it already is.

Try to recover quickly. One of you can say something that will calm the other one and make it easier to get back to connection.

You can also use this step to develop homework, building on whatever good happened in the session. For instance, if one partner calmed his arguing parts, you could suggest, "During the week, notice when your arguing parts emerge. Notice them before, during, or even after they get active. As we did today, notice them with gentleness, acknowledge their positive intentions, and ask them to step aside and let you handle it. Would you like set a goal of doing this a certain number of times this week? Would it work to mark it on a calendar or paper so you can see how many times you did it?"

Ongoing Sessions—Keeping Momentum and Focus

Successful IFS couples therapy depends on keeping the focus on parts and Self energy. Notice how couples veer off from this goal.

Recognize parts that may want to chat or talk "about" issues, and ask them if they will let you do something different. Be wary of saying things in the beginning that encourage people to chat or analyze.

Consider having both partners check in about what they want to address before focusing on any one issue. To me, it's like seeing the menu before ordering. You may also ask questions to set the intent for the meeting. For example, "Together, let's focus on our goal: that you have the best possible relationship." Or, "What is true, relevant, tender, or risky?" Use statements that help you and the couple focus on the highest intent of the meeting.

It's good to hear complaints between the partners because it helps you find the parts that create the stuck places between them. But once you hear the complaints, look for parts in the way of Self energy. Don't let complaint sessions go on too long.

Once you have a target part, avoid jumping from subject to subject. Stay focussed on this target part, even over multiple sessions, until it can relax and let Self lead. If you have focused on specific parts in the previous session, you may need to ask about them, especially if they were Exiles.

Aside from focusing on one partner to get to Exiles, you may find yourself interacting more with one partner than another in general. Try to find out why one partner is participating less.

You may feel at times that the therapy is not progressing. Perhaps you aren't looking forward to seeing the couple, or you feel distracted or tired during the sessions. It's good to pay attention to that. There could be valuable information in your body and your experience. You may find it useful to ask something like, "Do we have traction?" The couple's response may help get the therapy back on track or clarify why it can't progress. Sometimes you may be surprised to find an undisclosed secret or affair has been hindering the couples therapy.

As you spend more time with couples, unspoken communication deepens. Projection, transference, and counter-transference become richer. You and your parts can use all of this information to help the couple focus on their issues.

Three Things That Work in a Fight

As you read in Chapter 11, there are three things that work in a fight: the Do-Over, 100% Admitting, and Giving Better Back. Partners can use these methods at home to end fights and get back to connection and intimacy. You can use them in your office when couples come in fighting or when there isn't anything else to focus on in a particular session.

Unfortunately, there are many things that don't work in a fight. Once a fight has started, Firefighters are engaged. They have decided that the other partner is causing pain and they want it to stop. They are engaged with their best efforts: arguing, blaming, judging, educating, pleading, punishing, distancing, collapsing, and distracting. Once one partner's Firefighters start, the other partner's Firefighters join in. Both partners are trying to stop the pain, but not in a way that brings them back to the love they desire.

These three techniques work in a fight because they do one crucial thing: disarm Firefighters. They focus on taking responsibility for one's actions, admitting one's part, and giving. They offer no comments on what the other partner did wrong or how they could change. Firefighters are surprised and disarmed by this. Nothing negative or demanding is coming at them, so they have nothing to oppose. They can relax and let Self take over. That's when you see the fresh magic of gentleness, humor, compassion, and creativity.

These three techniques are structured ways to help one partner access Self energy while the other partner is engaged in inflammatory Firefighter activity. Once Self energy is present, outside structure is usually not needed, but in the confusing, distressing experience of fighting with your mate at home, structure can be a good way to get back on track.

To teach these methods in a couples therapy session, say, "I know you don't want to be in this fight. You both feel so much better when you are connected. Right now it's hard to get there. You're both trying your best, but it's not working. Would one of you like to try an experiment to end this fight? I'll explain it to you step by step."

Once you have a partner willing to try the experiment, listen for objections and engage with them respectfully. When you see doubt, hesitation, blankness, or confusion, say, "Maybe you have some reasons not to do this. What are they?" Once you have acknowledged objections (remember to do the heart flip), ask them to step aside and let the experiment proceed.

As part of your instructions, coach the "active" partner— the one doing the technique— to do the exercise and then stop talking. Otherwise they may get drawn into provocation. Explaining that they need to stop talking completely after they do their part is a way to avoid that. They can nod or acknowledge what their partner is saying, but they must not speak.

It's also important to prepare the active partners for negative results. No matter how well they do the exercise, the receiving partner probably won't relax right away. Their Firefighters may have noticed something different, but they may still want to test, resist, or provoke to see if the change is real and lasting. Also, it usually takes a while for receiving partners to wind down, even when they have received a beautiful, generous communication. Their protectors are spinning and momentum may keep them agitated for a while.

If the active partner is prepared for continued anger, attack, distance, or criticism, they'll have a better chance of staying in Self energy. The receiving partner will probably wind down within a couple of hours. Prepare the active partner for continued attack. Results are eventually profound and joyful.

Sometimes the receiving partner does not respond well, even after days have passed. Sometimes one partner can admit, do over, and give better back numerous times with no positive results. Is this a failure? No—because now the active partner has data. They know they did their best, and they can observe the results with calmness and clarity. Perhaps they will decide to continue, and perhaps they will decide, with peace and equanimity, that they want to end the relationship. Either way, they have more Self energy available.

Keep your focus on the active partner. These exercises help one partner get back to Self energy and stay there regardless of the provocation. Avoid the temptation to be "fair" and have both partners do the exercise. The purpose of these exercises is to help ONE partner access Self energy regardless of the other's behavior. There are three reasons to keep the focus on one partner:

1. The active partner benefits regardless of the results. The active partner is better off with calm, clarity, and connection than being consumed with Firefighter energy.

2. Time is limited, and it's most productive to use it to prepare the active partner for negative results. If the active partners are prepared, it's more likely they will stay in Self energy and benefit from their efforts. If you use session time to try to get both partners to do the exercise, you may not have time to do a thorough job with one of them.

3. This is better training for what happens at home. At home, they have no therapist to tell them to take turns. In the best situations, one partner gets a shred of Self energy, extracts themselves from Firefighter immersion, and tries one of the techniques. It's better for one partner to be prepared to do an exercise alone than have the unrealistic expectation that their companion will join them.

Giving Better Back

Giving Better Back can be the most powerful of the three techniques, but it takes longer to do. Self-like protectors and Managers often think it means being nice or giving in. You will need to address their ideas and ask them to let Self lead. There may be other parts that are afraid to let Self energy out if it is strong, clear, or courageous. You usually have to try a few times before you get a "better" response that is Self-led. Detailed instructions are in Chapter 6.

100% Admitting

100% Admitting is the quickest exercise to teach. The active partner admits to something he or she did to cause a problem or make things worse. They find a small thing they have done or said that they can admit caused or worsened the fight. They don't have to say or believe that they are solely responsible, but the admission has to be entirely about their contribution, with no reference to their partner.

The admitting has to be 100% to work. If there is anything that refers to the other partner, such as "because you made me," or "after you criticized me," or "not that you really care," or "just like you always do," the receiving partner's Firefighters will discount the admitting. You may have to talk to a few protectors before they give permission for this.

You can even use 100% Admitting to structure couples sessions when couples are not fighting. Explain the process and take a volunteer to admit a negative contribution for five to ten minutes. Next, switch to the other partner. You may say something like this:

> Since we don't have any specific plans for today, let's try an exercise to help you communicate more deeply. In this exercise, you will be taking turns, with one person talking and the other listening. The person who is talking thinks about the issue that brought you here and focuses only on their own part of it. Often, we think our partners are the main cause of the problem, or at least half of it. For this exercise, we take scissors and cut your partner completely out of the picture. You will talk only about your own contribution, even if it is just a tiny shred. Then, even if the listening partner argues or attacks, you will stick to your own part of it.

You may find that a few rounds of 100% Admitting deepen and increase communication, vulnerability, and tender expression. You may find that the conversation deepens with the second or third attempt.

In couples therapy sessions, these exercises can also be used to flush out parts that don't want to allow Self energy. For example, you can describe the 100% Admitting technique and then find that protective parts must see the other partner as attacking or dismissing, and that they are protecting young, wounded parts from experiencing this. This could be your opportunity to get to Exiles.

The Do Over

The Me Do-Over is often most useful at home. After you teach this exercise, you may hear happy stories of how partners used it on their own to stop fights or recover connection.

First, the active partner asks if it's okay to do a do-over. If the receiving partner says no, the exercise is postponed. If the answer is yes, the three steps that follow are "when, what, and stop."

First, the active partner describes the "when," the past experience they have in mind. Then, speaking in present tense, as if they were right back at that moment, the active partner says or does something different. For example, the active partner might say, "Remember when we were in the kitchen, and I said that you should wash the dishes for a change? Here is my do-over. 'Richard, would you be willing to do the dishes?'" That's the "what" portion of the do-over exercise. Then, as in all three exercises, the active partner stops talking, even if provoked. This is the "stop."

Endings and Ambiguous Commitment

The more you do couples therapy, the more likely you are to encounter couples who will separate. Often, you can help couples find their way back to love. Sometimes, however, it is not going to go that way. It's good to be alert for ambiguous commitment and related risky situations.

Sometimes it's not clear if a couple is going to stay together or separate. It's important to get as much clarity as you can about these situations. If they are talking about separating, or if you sense that they are thinking about it, ask tough questions and take the answers seriously. Their answers may determine how you approach the couples therapy or even if you agree to continue.

Here are some questions that might be helpful when commitment seems tenuous:

Why do you want to stay together?

If the answer to this question has nothing to do with love, the prognosis for couples therapy might not be good. In most cultures, people expect marriage to bring them the experience of love. This is a relatively recent development in the last one hundred and fifty years, but it is strongly engrained.

Couples might have good intentions to stay together for reasons other than love, but they are often insufficient. Being in couples therapy might make it even harder for them to stay together without love because honest conversation may make them face things they would rather ignore. If partners have really lost their love, and only want to stay together for children, financial security, or family approval, I usually question them further to see if there could still be love. If not, I may tell them I can't help them.

If people want to stay together because they love each other, or want to love each other, the prognosis for couples therapy is better. The important determinant is not how hard it is for people to be together, but how much they desire unity.

Are you ready to face the possibility of a separation or divorce?

If people believe they couldn't survive separation, it will be hard to have honest discussions. The fearful partner(s) may need to keep the therapy safe, non-confrontational, and ultimately, nonproductive. Perhaps you can help the partners find courage to face separation. With that courage, they will be able to have challenging discussions and possibly stay together. If not, it may be better to put couples therapy off for a while. Otherwise, you may find yourself wondering what they are getting out of the therapy. If you address this issue early, you can save yourself and them from an unproductive course of therapy.

Sometimes you may suspect that couples therapy isn't going anywhere. Perhaps you feel hopeless or tired before or during the session. Your low energy level could be giving you data about difficult commitment issues. If you ask questions, you may find out what parts are in the way of honesty. You may invite those parts to unblend and allow more Self energy to be present. For instance, ask, "Do we have traction? Are there questions we are not addressing? Are we avoiding something?"

It might seem obvious, but it's important to listen to disturbing statements. Sometimes we may want to tune them out, perhaps because we are rooting for the couple to stay together. Watch out for statement such as:

I really don't want this relationship anymore.

I just wanted to do couples therapy so I could say I tried everything.

I was hoping you could help my partner adjust to the end of the relationship.

I wish my partner would let me go.

These statements could mean there is not much hope for couples therapy. It's better to address them than to ignore them.

One Out of Two Is Really Done

Sometimes you know or suspect that one of the partners is really done with the relationship. Maybe they are saying so or maybe you sense it non-verbally. If there is any doubt, it's best to dive in and find the truth. If there are parts in the way of re-commitment, you could work with them. But if the decision has already been made, perhaps long ago, it could mean that there is little hope for productive couples therapy. If one partner has no love and no desire to feel love, there is little reason for him or her to work hard and reveal vulnerability in couples therapy.

If it becomes clear that one partner is done and ready to move on, it could be intensely disturbing for the partner that is still in love. Multiple protectors may come forth to try to "help" the situation. You may see vacillation between anger, grief, forcing, attack, victimhood, and hopelessness. In extreme situations, you may see suicidality. You may be able to help this partner release more Self energy to deal with their new reality, and/or you may suggest individual therapy or medication.

You may find that partners who are in love with someone who doesn't love them anymore are extremely motivated to recapture the love. They jump at the opportunity to work on their parts, give up lifelong addictions, and change according to the other partner's complaints.

Sometimes it does take the threat of loss to change bad habits. If the other partner is ready to separate, however, the most heroic efforts probably won't work. The out-of-love partner may have had years to silently let go, and they may have no interest in continuing, no matter what changes.

If the still-in-love partner agrees to focus on their parts to regain their companion's love, they may be very angry if their efforts are not rewarded. If you cooperate with this agenda, or even imply that working with their parts will result in getting their spouse back, they could feel used or betrayed if they do not succeed. If they think you misled them, they might even feel that they have a valid ethics charge.

You will be more effective and ethical if you let partners know that you are neutral about whether they stay together (see the next section on neutrality). The motivated partner may decide you are not the right therapist for them. It is better that they find someone else than agreeing to an unrealistic contract that may backfire and possibly put you at risk.

It may be better to focus on the non-loving partner and help them communicate their truth with clarity, confidence, and courage. Do they have parts holding them back from being direct and clear about the loss of love? Are they afraid of what would happen if they separated? Would they like to develop courage to speak their truth? They may benefit from individual sessions to get there, and they may want you to provide them. However, that could be risky for the other partner. Individual sessions might give them the courage to end the relationship, leaving the still-loving partner angry at you for "creating" a result that hurts them. If there is a divorce, the still-loving partners could draw you into a legal battle, and the individual sessions could make you ethically vulnerable.

When you do individual sessions, you have a fiduciary commitment to the individual client. When you do couples therapy, you have a fiduciary commitment to the couple. "Fiduciary" comes from the Latin word *fiducia*, which means trust. In psychotherapy, it means that the therapist has accepted the trust of the clients to act only for their benefit.

What if the couple and the individual partners have different ideas of benefit? If the couple is your client, they may agree that clarity and courage to face the truth, whatever it may be, will be the desired benefit. On the other hand, one partner may say yes to truth while the other wants to change the truth. If one of the partners is your client, he or she may believe that keeping the family intact is of benefit.

Lawyers could make the argument that acting for the benefit of one of the partners is in conflict with acting for the benefit of the couple, and you could be vulnerable to ethical or malpractice complaints. If you are aware of all this, and still think it's clinically advisable to meet individually, talk to the partners about the risks of individual sessions and document their responses. If their responses indicate that they don't understand or don't accept the risks, don't meet individually. You may also want to consult with the legal counsel for your professional organization.

The rule I use now is that I do individual sessions if the purpose is to reconnect. If the purpose of the individual session is to separate, I do not meet individually.

Be Neutral about the Outcome

Therapists should be neutral about whether a couple stays together. Without neutrality, it is hard to be present and welcoming to all the parts in the room. If you advocate for one result, you may find yourself pushing people rather than helping them find their own direction. The less you are driven by your own agenda, the more you will have access to your own Self energy and the capacity to help partners find what's right for them.

Tell the couple that this is your approach, especially if one of them is anxious to make the relationship work. This will give them the information they need to decide whether you are the right therapist for them. Prepare for a storm of protest from your own parts, and reassure them that it's best to be upfront about who you are, even if it means the couple leaves you.

When Couples Are Separating or Divorcing

Couples counseling can help partners end their relationship well. It can help both partners express themselves without guilt, blame, or shame, and can provide the opportunity to experience shared grief and sadness. This can set the stage for freedom and peace after divorce. It can result in reduced emotional baggage and a better ability to work together as co-parents.

There are a few sticky situations you may encounter when you do couples therapy with divorcing couples. You may find that one partner is really done, and the other is surreptitiously using couples therapy as a last ditch attempt to save the marriage. Perhaps the partner who is done is unclear and inconsistent about their intention to end the relationship, giving false hope.

It's best to find out as soon as possible whether the "done" partner is truly done, and if so, help them be clear, courageous, and confident about their decision. If you proceed as if the goal is reconciliation and it doesn't work, the hopeful partner may feel misled and become very angry. Once you get a clear answer from the partner who is ready to divorce, you can openly ask the other partner if they want couples therapy to help them get through the ending. Then they know why they are in therapy and can freely agree or decline.

You may meet divorcing couples who want to work on their intimate emotional relationship as if they were still together. Sometimes both partners believe that they should do this. It's best to tell them that once the decision to divorce has been made, it's best to focus on a good ending and not on building more emotional intimacy. Working on deepening intimacy could keep them from moving on, build false hope, and ultimately cause them to feel unsafe, since the container of a committed relationship is gone. Of course, people continue to grow emotionally after a divorce, but that is best done with their friends, individual therapists, in solitude, or with new partners.

More frequently, one partner wants to deepen intimacy and the other one doesn't. Perhaps one partner has felt the relationship is over for a long time and has only recently told the other, who is shocked. The shocked partner may still be in love and want the couples therapy as a lifeline in an extremely disorienting situation.

Despite the agreed upon end of the relationship, one partner may still hope that the relationship can continue. They may be willing to uncover vulnerabilities, thinking it will help get their partner back. The partner who is done may also comply with deep parts work out of guilt. Underneath this willingness, there may be a latent, unspoken feeling of vulnerability or danger. It's up to you to help them understand that opening up may not be in their best interest.

The desire to keep growing intimately after divorce can also be a way to avoid facing grief and loss. A relationship is a living thing, like a person, and when it's over, it's complete and it dies, much as a human life is complete at the time of death. It's important to relate fully with the ending, feel it, accept it, and move on to a different relationship with the ex-spouse. Avoiding this process could prolong the period of adjustment, even creating long-lasting problems and impacting future relationships.

You may want to make it clear to separating couples that you won't be helping them look at parts that are in the way of intimacy with each other. You may tell them that you believe the relationship is complete and you hope they continue to grow individually. However, you recommend they grow on their own, with their individual therapists, or at some point, with their future new partners.

Post-separation couples therapy may not last long. Perhaps a couple is reluctant to leave you when they are leaving each other, and they just need a few more sessions. Perhaps they doubt that they can stay reasonable as they work out the separation details and they want your support while they gain confidence. Perhaps one partner is not as prepared as the other for the loss of the relationship, and a few more sessions would be comforting.

The couple may ask you to shift from deep couples therapy to coaching about co-parenting. Can you make the change? If you are only interested in deeply experiential couples therapy, as I am, this may be very difficult. I've tried it, and I found myself inevitably slipping back toward deep parts work. I've learned I need to keep it brief when partners have agreed on divorce, refer to parenting coaches and mediators, and say goodbye as soon as the couple can tolerate it.

You may encounter a situation in which one of the partners is overtly or covertly suicidal. Consider referring that person to an individual therapist as a condition for couples therapy. Once you start, it could be hard to leave someone who is in such deep need, and you may lose your opportunity to be available to the couple if they should ever need you in the future.

Working with Your Own Parts

As always, watch for the obscuration of Self energy within yourself. Couples who are unclear or misaligned about ending their relationship may trigger parts of you that think you have to help, that don't want to feel sadness and loss, or who fear that the couple will judge you for not helping. Remind your parts that you don't have to help everyone. You can gently say no to things that your wisdom tells you won't work well, and you can tolerate judgment. Witnessing sadness can be a great service. It can be a poignant, inspiring experience to be present with couples when they mourn their relationship. You can help them move on, feel peace, and know they ended their relationship well.

Affairs: Six Steps to Healing

Couples can heal from affairs. The process can be heart-breaking, poignant, fiery, slow, difficult, and imperfect, but it can happen.

The six steps below will help you navigate post-affair couples therapy. Many of these steps come from training with Sunny Shulkin, master Imago Relationship therapist and trainer. Sunny can be found on the Imago Relationship Therapy website.

Some of the steps are necessary because of the divergent experiences of the two partners. Since one had an affair and the other didn't (at least at the time of the therapy), they usually differ in trust, vulnerability, level of distress, and knowledge. The therapy can't be equal in the beginning because their experiences aren't equal. One way to deal with this is to start the therapy with an emphasis on the affair partner (the one who had the affair).

What Kind of Affair Was It?

Before you get started, it's important to know what kind of affair occurred. There are different issues in different kinds of affairs. The partners themselves might not know what kind of affair it was and may be making unfounded assumptions. To put it in context, you may need to know if the couple had a clear monogamy contract or some other kind of contract, such as "don't get caught" or "not with my best friend."

Was it a one night stand with no emotional involvement and

no ongoing contact? In this case, you won't have to deal with the affair partner being in love with another person.

Was it one of a series of affairs over a period of time? Perhaps this was the first time someone was caught, or the second or third. If there is a long standing pattern of affairs in one person in a monogamous marriage, the person who has the affairs may be resistant to change. They may say they want to be faithful but have parts that do not want to stop. Be careful about making a realistic contract.

Did the affair partner fall in love? Is he or she still in love? You may not know at first. Some people will not tell the whole truth. Perhaps the partner who fell in love in an affair wants to fall out of love and come back to the marriage. You may be able to help with that.

Or maybe the affair partner wants to stay in love and isn't saying so. They might be afraid that it will hurt their partner or end the marriage. Perhaps they are coming to couples therapy because of the betrayed partner's wishes, because they need time before they are ready to say they are done, or because they want you to help prepare the faithful partner for the end. Maybe they are waiting for favorable conditions, such as a child navigating a milestone or a financial event.

Perhaps they know that ending the marriage will be a contentious, frightening process, and they do not yet have the courage. Sometimes people don't have financial resources to leave, or they are worried about custody or co-parenting after a divorce.

Use your intuition. If you feel something is missing or unspoken, it may be so. Even as you ask direct, challenging questions, you can still be gentle, curious, and non-judgmental.

The Affair Partner Does More Work in the First Four Steps

Faithful partners are often dealing with betrayal, loss of trust, disorientation, shock, despair, and uncertainty about the future.

They may not know whether they can or even want to heal from the affair. Unlike the betrayed partner, they know everything that happened in the affair because they were there. They may be holding back some details and may be conflicted about who they love. Affair partners often want to move on and forget the affair, skip over remorse, and focus on improving the relationship. However, it may be too soon for the betrayed partner.

Affair partners often have work to do before the faithful partner joins in as an equal participant. It's best that they understand that the faithful partner is probably too vulnerable to reveal their own parts and do much of their own work in the beginning of couples therapy.

Step One: The Affair Is Totally Over

The first step is making sure the affair is over. If the affair partner is still in love or involved with the other person, the faithful partner is probably not safe enough to open up and be vulnerable. Some faithful partners may say they feel safe and want to risk working on their own parts. It's worth exploring before you plunge in, because the faithful partner may be unaware of how vulnerable and insecure they actually are. They may want to override these feelings out of fear of losing their partner, but there could be a backlash of anger and betrayal if it doesn't work. It's often best to discourage faithful partners from being vulnerable, revealing hurt Exiles, or participating as an equal in couples therapy until the affair is truly over.

The affair partner may want to process relationship issues with the faithful partner right away, but it's often better to discourage that until the affair is over. Processing involves both partners being vulnerable, and it is not fair or safe to ask the faithful partner to do that while an affair is active.

It can be complicated to find out if an affair is concluded. The affair partner may have had intimate, heartfelt feelings for the other person, and they may not end on schedule or demand. The affair partner may not want the relationship to end and may or may not be honest about that.

If a couple starts couples therapy with an affair still ongoing, there are reasons to question whether the affair will ever end. Since the affair partner started the affair, continued it after the faithful partner found out, and continues it even while starting couples therapy, there must be strong reasons for its existence. If that's the case, couples therapy is probably not indicated. Individual therapy for each partner may be more beneficial.

It may be clinically advisable to do individual sessions with the partners while the affair is still going on, but it is probably not legally or ethically advisable. Since an ongoing affair makes divorce and legal involvement more likely, it's best to think ahead about what lawyers might do. They may attack you for doing both individual and couples therapy, discounting your argument that you did it to help the couple's therapy. One or both of the partners may make ethical complaints. It's better to refer for individual therapy when divorce is a strong possibility. It is wise to consult your profession's legal counsel. At the very least, discuss and document the purpose and risk of individual sessions with the partners.

Sometimes the affair partner says the affair is over and the faithful partner has doubts. You can often rely on the faithful partner's intuition. If they don't believe it's over, it's quite possible that it isn't. Often the only way the truth comes out is if the faithful partner finds evidence. I neither encourage nor discourage faithful partners from seeking evidence of the relationship in the affair partners' cell phones or credit card receipts.

Sometimes you may wonder why the faithful partner does not express suspicions. You may need to explore why they don't want to ask questions or take the answers seriously. They may have parts holding them back. If they are not addressed in the beginning, the couples therapy may stagnate.

Perhaps you have suspicions. You might need to confront the affair partner with direct, probing questions.

Also, remember that affair partners often minimize their past or current affair involvement. Watch for statements such as "It's over for now...I have feelings for....We met once or twice...There wasn't much physical intimacy..." Such statements can mask greater intimate involvement.

You may be concerned that your questions will sound judgmental. As always, do the heart flip before you speak. If you are judging someone for having an affair, not ending an affair, or being evasive, don't say a word until you get your judging parts to step aside. You can be very direct if you don't judge.

Step Two: They Want to Heal from the Affair

Do both partners want to heal from the affair? Try to discern their intentions. If one of them doesn't want to heal from the affair and embrace the challenges of the marriage, there might not be a reason to go too far into the affair issues. If the affair has led one or both to lose connection, and they really don't want to get it back, it's best to face the truth. Healing from an affair is arduous, demanding, and sometimes heart-breaking, and it might not be worth the effort if one or both do not want to stay together.

Step Three: There Is Real Remorse

It's important that the affair partner expresses remorse. The faithful partner usually needs it to move on. They need to know that their partner knows how much they've been hurt and regrets their part in it. So much of the wounding of being betrayed is about being ignored, unmet, uncared for, unwanted, and disenfranchised. Remorse is an experience that binds the partners together and allows faithful partners to feel seen and understood.

Affair partners also benefit from feeling and expressing remorse. They may have parts that want to deny it happened or think of it as a crazy aberration that will never happen again. Feeling and expressing remorse might make it hard to maintain denial. Or perhaps parts already feel so guilty that they fear that remorse will make them sink into a pit of guilt and shame. Maybe they think they need to shield themselves from the effects of their actions because they would be judgmental of themselves if they really faced it.

By avoiding remorse, they are avoiding honesty about what they did and the opportunity to feel free of guilt. They may also have burdened and disempowered themselves with lies and deceit, and remorse and truth telling can relieve that. Remorse is a more relational feeling than guilt, shame, or denial and can help bring the couple back together. Remorse is usually more Self-led, and guilt and shame are more parts-led.

Step Four: The Affair Partner Answers Questions about Details

The affair partner and the faithful partner differ in their knowledge of what happened. The affair partner knows what happened because they were there. The faithful partner doesn't know what happened and may default to imagining a wide range of events. In order to prune their imagining to a better approximation of reality, they need information.

Be sure to advise the faithful partner to choose their questions carefully. They will have to live with the answers. Hopefully they can discern what information they need in order to move on and what information, if spoken, would haunt them for years to come. Try to help the faithful partners question wisely.

This questioning is usually irritating for the person who had the affair. They know what happened and they want to move on. Sharing details can feel like reliving the past. They may be afraid to hurt the faithful partner. But they need to understand that the faithful partner may not be able to move on until they know what they are moving on from. Here is what many faithful partners say after they get the details they wanted:

> Now I know. It was important for me to know. It was everything and now it's just what it was. I don't have to guess or have doubts

> that will get in the way of going forward. It's all clear. There's no information that I don't have that I'm going to worry about. It's all out there.

Some experts believe it's best to leave out the details, spare the faithful partner the hurt of knowing what happened, and move on. This approach fails to recognize the different experiences and needs of the two partners.

Step Five: The Faithful Partner Regains Trust

Affair partners need to prove to the faithful partners that they are trustworthy, and the faithful partners need to accept this and regain trust. It may take time for the faithful partner to trust again. The affair partner may need to do things to help the faithful partner regain trust. Some faithful partners benefit from regular check-ins about routine contact with the affair person or clear agreements about what the affair partner will do if there is any contact. The affair partners probably won't want to do this, since they already know what contact there is or isn't, and they don't understand that the faithful partner lacks this information. They may also wish the faithful partners would just drop it. Again, they need to understand that experiences are different, and they may need to do extra work to advance the healing process.

Sometimes the faithful partner cannot regain trust even though they want to. You may find yourself making invitations to faithful partners to get to know their untrusting parts, but be careful about how safe it is for them to reveal their vulnerability.

Step Six: Partners Address Relationship Issues as Equals

It is now safe for the affair partners to bring up their own issues about the marriage, and couples therapy can become more equal. Both partners are now looking for parts and becoming vulnerable in front of each other.

Therapist Parts in Affair Situations

Affairs can easily bring up judgmental parts. If you judge either partner, you cannot be effective or helpful. As always, do the heart flip with any judging parts you may have.

Because affair couples are often in such pain and distress, you may feel more pressured to help than usual. Be careful—you may not know what help they need at first. For example, the partners may say they want help reconnecting and healing, but that may not be the whole truth. Don't let your parts jump in too far before you know what they need.

Special Issues in Couples Therapy

There are probably as many special issues in couples therapy as there are couples. Each couple is unique. Your Self energy will help you meet new, unforeseen, and ambiguous situations.

As you see more couples, you may notice particular issues that keep coming up. Here are a few I have noticed:

Rage
Here I am addressing the issue of raging during a couples therapy session, not the issue of rage or violence at home. That can be abusive and dangerous, and it requires a different approach which may not include couples therapy. Couples therapists should be aware of the latest research on domestic violence, the danger signals, and recommended treatment. At the least, be aware that many experts believe that couples therapy is not indicated when there is violence at home.

The IFS approach to rage during a therapy session is simple, elegant, and effective. People who are raging have parts that need to rage, and once you find the parts, help them unblend, and facilitate parts-Self dialogue, you and the person will find out why the part thinks it has to rage. You will have the opportunity to address Exiles behind the rage. Once the raging parts are understood in this non-aggressive, relational way, and Exiles are unburdened, people will have more control over their rage.

Raging parts in a couples therapy session do damage and take time away from productive activity. It's best to address them quickly, before the other partner is hurt, and before the conversation gets so broken that it will take a long time to get back to connection.

"Frontloading" a conversation is helpful in avoiding raging interchanges in your office. Frontloading means loading up the work you do with partners as soon as possible, maybe even before they begin to speak. Frontloading is especially helpful when raging Firefighters have come out in previous conversations, and you anticipate that they will appear. Frontloading can be a much better use of your time than repairing the damage after raging occurs. You may even spend most of the session frontloading and have only five minutes of dialogue between the partners, but it will be good, safe dialogue.

The work of frontloading mostly involves finding and dialoguing with parts that want to rage. Sometimes just acknowledging the parts and asking them to step aside will be enough. Other times you may need to proceed to unburdening.

Raging parts, like all parts, are good and have good intentions. Here are a few examples of what raging parts have said to Self:

"I have to keep you from looking stupid."

"I have to make sure you act like a real man, because otherwise, you won't be attractive."

"I have to make her stop belittling you. You were demolished in childhood, and I won't let it happen again."

"You have to be on guard. If you don't attack, you will be attacked."

Most of the time, partners can access their raging parts in front of each other, and that is preferable in couples therapy. Sometimes they need the partner to leave the room or have a completely separate session.

You may find that you respond to men's and women's rage differently. As always, pay attention to your parts. If you find yourself fearful or reluctant to focus on raging parts, look inside yourself for the reason. Here are some triggers I have found:

The verbal volume of men's rage and the physical power of the person delivering it

Men's entitlement or justification for their rage

Women alternating between rage and victimhood

Women feeling unsupported if you question their rage

Avoiding or over-reacting to the potential for violence at home

Traumatized Partners
Couples therapy can be complicated when one or both partners have been traumatized. Some of the issues may be more extreme. For instance, you may find that partners are leading very distant lives, with little connection, enjoyment, or sex. They may be raging destructively at each other, or they may have settled into a victim/abuser pattern. While it is sad to see people who want to love each other act coldly or aggressively toward each other, it is possible that these extreme kinds of behaviors are actually helping the couple stay together, and making their relationship, even if extremely limited, possible. Be aware of any parts you might have that interpret or judge the way a couple is living.

When Exiles have been so badly hurt by trauma, Firefighters and Managers need to be particularly active. They are responsible for extreme distance or aggression. It's important to recognize that protectors act out of love and perceived need. You will probably need to find and acknowledge protectors who think they need to act in an extreme fashion. If you can meet reactive parts and find out what they are doing, they will feel understood and may be willing to modify their activities. You can do this with direct access or Self-part interactions. Even though these parts are explosive, they are often willing to work with Self if their concerns are addressed. As always, find the protectors and appreciate them, and make your way to Exiles as soon as you can.

It may be harder than usual for some traumatized partners to listen calmly to each other and to respond compassionately after one of them has opened up and revealed vulnerable parts. You may find that you have done everything you can to prepare one partner to listen while you focus on the other. The individual listens calmly while you do tender Exile work with the other person, and then they shock you with provocative, attacking statements at the end. That's an awful experience for the partner who just exposed tender parts. It's better not to do this kind of work than to have something hurtful happen at the end.

With traumatized partners, it may be harder for you to assess the partners' ability to be supportive with each other. You may check in with the other partner and they may say or look like they can be present, but then they erupt at the end of the session. They may have parts that think they have to go along or be "good" and other parts that want to take over afterward and blast their companion. Sometimes, Self-like parts make it hard for you to find polarities until they erupt. Traumatized people often have very good masks to help them look normal, making it hard for you to read them. Their parts may be separate enough that even they are unaware that they are going to erupt.

Because of these issues, it's often a good idea to leave a lot of time at the end of a session to deal with surprise attacks, even if you think you won't need it. Sometimes the best you can do is to warn the partners that sessions may not always end on a calm note and put supports in place between sessions.

Most of us have parts that want our partner to heal our wounds, but they can be more dedicated and extreme in traumatized individuals. Watch for unrelenting complaints, expectations, and rage about the other partner's behavior. Try to find these parts, validate their protective intent, and show them that healing comes from Self, not the other partner.

Traumatized partners can be abusive toward each other. They may be repeating learned attachment or relational patterns or just trying to get the other partner to understand how much they hurt. You must find and relate to the abusing parts through direct access or Self–part interactions. If not, couples therapy will be damaging. If the abuse can't stop, couples therapy may not be indicated.

Feedback: Healthy and Hazardous

As you read in Chapter 10, "Feedback: The Other Side of the Coin," feedback is hazardous to the partner who gives it. No matter how well a partner expresses feedback, they probably won't get an ideal response. It's difficult to receive feedback, especially from a partner, and hardly anyone responds well at first. As one receiver of feedback said to me, "I feel like a baby seal being clubbed. It feels like I have to be a saint to take it in without throwing it back." The giver of feedback needs to be prepared to weather waves of defensiveness and be ready to stay in Self energy throughout the whole conversation.

When you notice that feedback has started, it's often best to focus on the person giving the feedback. You can help them give it with Self energy and continue throughout ensuing Firefighter responses.

You may want to help the giver of feedback use "I" statements and be gentle, curious, and clear. However, no matter how well the feedback is given, there is no guarantee that the response will be good. It's often better to spend more time preparing for Firefighter responses than on instructing people on the best way to give feedback. If they are in Self energy, it will be given well, even if it's not worded exactly right, and they will be better prepared for negative outcomes.

Surprisingly, positive feedback can create the same difficulties as negative feedback. Partners can be sweetly appreciative and surprised when it doesn't work well. Protectors may take compliments as threats. They may think, "Why didn't you say this before? You're too late. You don't mean it. You don't value me," and begin their attacks. Partners giving compliments should be prepared for difficult responses. Then they can maintain their positive intent and avoid contributing to disconnection. If they are able to do this, the receiving partner may wind down and eventually receive the compliment.

Good Luck in Your IFS Couples Therapy Work

Helping couples eliminate suffering and enjoy happiness is a rewarding endeavor. You will see people in their realness and rawness, their compassion and cruelty, and in all shades of protective energy. Seeing Self energy dawn in the midst of suffering will benefit them, you, their children, their friends, and beyond. It's worth it.

Coda

Bravo! You have learned about a new approach to relation-ships. You can turn it upside down and change attack, blame, and distance into compassion, calm, and connection. You have the courage to admit, "If it's intense, it's my own." You know how to focus on your protective parts when they get extreme, acknowledging and appreciating their efforts. You have found the possibilities that arise when your protectors step aside and let your true self interact with your partner. You welcome the challenges your relationship brings you, knowing that meeting them enriches you as a person. You have had moments of delightful surprise when dreary patterns changed in a flash to connection, humor, and compassion. You have felt the resonance of feedback given and received. You have felt gratitude and awe for the unique web of connection between you and your partner.

APPENDIX A
Self Qualities

Curiosity

Calm

Compassion

Confidence

Courage

Clarity

Connectedness

Creativity

Outline of the IFS Couples Process

Following is an outline of the process described in this book.

1. You have a desire for a loving relationship with your partner.
2. You notice a difficult interaction with your partner.
3. You become aware of your own protective parts (Managers and Firefighters) taking over.
    a. You can become aware of protectors by looking for blaming, shaming, collapsing, distancing, disconnection, hopelessness, judgment, anger, etc.
    b. You can become aware of protectors when you notice that one or more Self qualities are missing.
4. You approach your protective part with curiosity and respect.
5. You discover the logic of your protective part.
    a. Your protective part tells you why it's protecting you.
    b. Your protective part tells you what bad thing would happen if it didn't protect you.
6. You acknowledge your protector part for its good efforts and its beliefs.
7. You connect with the Exile behind the protector. If there was no Exile, there would be no need to protect.
8. You stay with the Exile, offering attention, validation, and connection until it relaxes.

9. You go back to the interaction with your partner with connection, compassion, clarity, confidence, courage, curiosity, calm, and creativity.
10. You give better back than you were getting. You respond to your partner with more Self qualities than you are getting.

References

Barbera, M. (2001). Projective Redemption in Couples Therapy: Interrupting Projective Identification Cycles. *Journal of Psychoanalysis and Psychotherapy*, 18:171-192

Barbera, M. (2005). Contemporary Psychoanalytic Relational Theory and Imago: Concepts for Relational Healing. In W. Luquet, H. Hendrix, M. Hannah, & H. Hunt, (Eds.), *Imago Relationship Therapy: Perspectives on Theory* (pp. 122-136). San Francisco: Jossey Bass

Chodron, P. (1991). *The Wisdom of No Escape.* Boston, MA: Shambhala Publications

Gottman, J. and Silver, N. (1999). *Seven Principles for Making Marriage Work.* New York: Three Rivers Press

Hendrix, H. (1988). *Getting the Love You Want.* New York: Henry Holt and Company

Lewis, T., Amini, F, & Lannon, R. (2000). *A General Theory of Love.* New York: Vintage Books

Luquet, W., Hannah, M., & Hunt, H. (2005). *Imago Relationship Therapy: Perspectives on Theory*. San Francisco: Jossey-Bass

Perel, E. (2006). *Mating in Captivity: Reconciling the Erotic and the Domestic*. New York: HarperCollins Publishers

Schwartz, R. (1995). *Internal Family Systems Therapy*. New York: Guilford Press

Schwartz, R. (2001). *Introduction to the Internal Family Systems Model*. Oak Park, Illinois: The Center for Self Leadership

Schwartz, R. (2004). The Larger Self. *Psychotherapy Networker*, May/June, 37-43

Schwartz, R. (2008). *You Are the One You've Been Waiting For*. Oak Park, Illinois: The Center for Self Leadership

Simmer-Brown, J. (2001). *Dakini's Warm Breath*. Boston, MA: Shambhala Publications

Smith, M.L. (2004). *A Season for the Spirit: Readings for the Days of Lent*. New York: Seabury Classics

Trungpa, C. (1988). *The Sacred Path of the Warrior*. Boston, MA: Shambhala Publications

Index

functioning of, 16, 27-31, 42, 110, 122
in couples therapy, 145
influence partner choice, 87–89
live in old pain, 14, 41
taking care of, 29, 72, 52-54
Sarah's, 7-8
what they are, 14, 87
what they want, 29, 87

F

feedback, see also exercises
after you give feedback, 118, 123
and Self qualities, 112–120
before giving feedback, 122
dangers of, 110, 123,
fear, 117
guilt, 118
preparing for, 119–126
what is good feedback, 107–108, 111–112
Firefighters
addictive, 102
angry, 93-96
arguing, 97
characteristics of, 15, 16, 58, 105
contemptuous, 96
distancing, 97
getting to know your, 17–20
hopeless and resigned, 99
identifying, 16–17

illustrations of, 14–15
influence partner choice, 89–90
lecturing, 100–101
moralizing, 100
noticing, 17–18
purpose, 15, 76, 95
punishing, 101–102
righteous, 100
self-harming, 103
value of understanding, 20, 105
what is your Firefighter protecting, 20
forcing, 103–104

G

giving better back
as a way of life, 72
defined, 55, 59–60
Elizabeth's story, 57-58
exercise, 70–72
Maria and John's story, 62-63
practical tool, 55
Raphael and Courtney's story, 66-69
with connection, 64
your natural state, 65
Gottman, J., 96, 100, 141

H

Hendrix, Harville, 145
hopelessness, 151, 152, 194, 195

ABOUT THE AUTHOR

MONA BARBERA, PH.D is a licensed psychologist practicing in Middletown, RI and Providence, RI. She specializes in couples therapy and provides workshops for couples and couples therapists. She is an Assistant Trainer for Internal Family Systems. After a few years as a struggling actress, she received her B.A in psychology from Antioch West, her M.Ed. from the University of Vermont, and her Ph.D. from New York University. She has written academic articles on couples for publications including *The Journal of Imago Relationship Therapy* and *The Journal of Psychoanalysis and Psychotherapy*, and a chapter in *Imago Relationship Therapy: Perspectives on Theory*, by Luquet, Hannah, and Hunt. She is past chair of the program committee and past board member of the New England Society for the Study and Treatment of Trauma and Dissociative Disorders. She lives in Rhode Island with her husband.

For more information about Mona Barbera's tapes, workshops, and teaching schedule, please contact:

Dos Monos Press
341 Broadway
Providence, RI 02909

or visit: www.monabarbera.com

ABOUT INTERNAL FAMILY SYSTEMS

Internal Family Systems^{SM} therapy, founded by Richard Schwartz, Ph.D, is at the forefront of a movement in psychotherapy toward a more collaborative approach that relies on clients' intuitive wisdom. As one of the fastest growing approaches in the field today, it has had a significant impact on the field of psychotherapy. Internal Family Systems (IFS) offers a clear, non-pathologizing and empowering method of understanding human problems that is becoming widely embraced by the trauma community and by those interested in integrating spirituality with psychotherapy. It offers a philosophy of practice that allows both the therapist and client to enter a transformational relationship in which healing occurs.

The Center for Self Leadership is dedicated to the healing transformation of lives and cultures through educating therapists, health care professionals, and the public in the IFS psychotherapeutic model. For information and resources such as training programs, lists of IFS therapists, retreats, conferences, workshops, dvds, books, bibliography, Journal of Self Leadership, and IFS personality scale, visit www.selfleadership.org

Lightning Source UK Ltd.
Milton Keynes UK
UKHW020820121222
413794UK00016B/1081